International Business

SAGE COURSE COMPANIONS
KNOWLEDGE AND SKILLS *for* SUCCESS

International Business

Gabriele Suder

Los Angeles • London • New Delhi • Singapore • Washington DC

First published 2009

SAGE Publications Ltd
1 Oliver's Yard
55 City Road
London EC1Y 1SP

SAGE Publications Inc.
2455 Teller Road
Thousand Oaks, California 91320

SAGE Publications India Pvt Ltd
B 1/I 1 Mohan Cooperative Industrial Area
Mathura Road, Post Bag 7
New Delhi 110 044

SAGE Publications Asia-Pacific Pte Ltd
33 Pekin Street #02-01
Far East Square
Singapore 048763

Library of Congress Control Number: 2008929531

British Library Cataloguing in Publication data

A catalogue record for this book is available from the British Library

ISBN 978-1-4129-3104-5
ISBN 978-1-4129-3105-2 (pbk)

Typeset by C&M Digitals (P) Ltd., Chennai, India
Printed in India by Replika Press Pvt Ltd.
Printed on paper from sustainable resources

contents

Acknowledgements   vii

Part One   Introduction to your IB companion   1

Part Two   Core areas of the IB curriculum   9

             Introduction to the running themes in the book   9

2.1   International Business basics: terminologies and first
       reflections on globalization, regionalism and
       international commerce   11
2.2   International trade and investment theory   16
2.3   Foundations of international economy and trade:
       culture, politics, law and ethics   26
2.4   Economic integration and trade relations   39
2.5   Globalization and the monetary system   47
2.6   Internationalization: theory, tools and HR issues   56
2.7   International strategy and organizational structures   66
2.8   Business operations and international marketing   75
2.9   Risk and uncertainties   87
2.10   Knowledge management in international business   99
2.11   The international economy and international trade
       or: Why and how is international business
       influenced by the global policy environment?   112

Part Three   Study, writing and revision skills
               (in collaboration with David McIlroy)   123

3.1.   How to get the most out of your lectures   124
3.2.   How to make the most of seminars   129
3.3.   Essay writing tips   134
3.4.   Revision hints and tips   144
3.5.   Exam tips   155
3.6.   Tips on interpreting essay and exam questions   165

Part Four   Essential resources   179

Glossary   180
Bibliography   190
Appendix of useful websites   195
Index   197

acknowledgements

The author would like to express her thanks and love to David, Chantal and Caroline, as well as to Ingrid and Rudolf.

Also, many thanks to Delia Alfonso, Anne Summers, Clare Wells and Jennifer Pegg at Sage for their professionalism, and to the reviewers for their valuable comments and suggestions. Part Three is part of Sage's standard companion guide text and was adapted for this book; all credentials go to its author.

Thank you for the assistance of, in particular, Cecile Klawatsch and Marek Turkiewicz, at the final stages of the manuscript's proofreading.

Gabriele Suder

part one
introduction to your IB companion

This international business book is part of the series of Sage Course Companions. The companions are designed to optimise your studies and your learning, to facilitate your comprehensions and to help you prepare for lectures, exams and what follows: the role of an international business manager. This series is an essential 'take away' from your studies. It is a reference and guide to your subject, with short, clear, crucial information about your topic, plus an indication of trends that are part of business evolutions. The aim is to help you be successful in your studies and work.

Your lecturers will most commonly decide upon a particular, traditional, most often rather lengthy textbook for your course in international business. The typical textbook is useful as it provides great detail, illustrations and case studies, exercises and much material that may nonetheless make you doubt what is essential and what is not. In this somewhat overwhelming situation, Sage Course Companions provide you with a straightforward guide that summarizes the essentials of the subject, their interrelationships and background. You will gain an insider's overview of your course that will enable you to fill in detail as required, and explains key concepts to foster your understanding of the essentials. It supports you with knowledge that is handily available to help write your essays and assignments and for passing your exams.

If you buy this Companion at the beginning of your course, it will remain with you like a good friend, and serve in parallel with your course texts and lectures. It is not going to replace your textbook, but it will save you time when you are revising for your exams or preparing course work. Written by an experienced international business professor, the Companion is conceived as a guideline on what your examiners will be looking for; it is a framework in which to apply your critical thinking, with indications to where current trends lead.

Introducing your companion

This companion covers the most important points from your textbooks, lecture notes, and other learning materials on your course, and should be used as a complement or a learning facilitator. This book should direct you to the key issues in the field of international business. No matter which textbook you are using, the main tools and concepts are the same: indeed, you will find references to some specific books, and where they cover the themes elaborated here; again, you should read the Companion in parallel with your textbook and identify where subjects are covered in more detail in both your text and in your course syllabus, in order to train with this material.

There is also a study and revision skills guide in Part Three which will help you to learn more efficiently. Learning is best accomplished by seeing the information from several different angles, which is why you attend lectures and tutorials, read the textbook, and read around the subject in general. This book will help you to bring together these different sources.

How to use this book

Ideally, you should have already bought this book before your course starts, so that you can get a quick overview of each topic before you go into the lecture – but if you didn't do this, all is not lost. The Companion will still be equally helpful as a revision guide, and as a way of directing you to the key concepts, tools and some of the key thinkers in international business.

This first section is about the fundamentals of international business: it will help you to get into the mindset of the subject and think about it critically. Examiners want to see that you can handle the basic concepts of the subject: if you need a quick overview of the background to international business, this is the section you will find most useful.

The next section goes into the curriculum in more detail, taking each topic and providing you with the key elements. Again, this does not substitute for the deeper coverage you will have had in your lectures and texts, but it does provide a quick revision guide, or a 'primer' to use before lectures. It will also give you ideas about the issues that will typically be explored when going further than the textbook.

You can use this book either to give yourself a head start before you start studying international business – in other words, to give yourself a preview course – or it can be used as a revision aid, or of course both. As appropriate, the sections contain the following features:

- Tips on handling the knowledge, or the way in which your examiner will most likely ask the questions in that section, to help you to anticipate exam questions.
- Bullet points that help you remember the main points to bring in when answering exam questions.
- Examples: these are useful for putting the theory into a 'real-world' context, and can of course be used in exams to illustrate the points you make.
- Quotes from key thinkers or key organizations in the field: these will be useful to quote in exams, as well as providing you with the main influences in the development of international business.
- Sample exam questions with indications for the answers: these should help you be better prepared for the actual questions, even though they will (of course) be different.
- Taking it Further section: this is about taking your learning and thinking a stage beyond simply laying out the current 'received wisdom'. The Taking it Further section introduces some criticality, often from 'sharp end' academic thinking, or gives further insight into a topic for better understanding, and will help you to take a broader conceptual view of the topic: on a practical level, this is the type of knowledge and thinking that moves you from a pass to a first!

Part Three of this Companion is a study guide which will help you with getting more from your lectures, remembering more when you are sitting exams, and with writing essays. A glossary of key terms is included at the back of the book. Key terms are defined so that they are easy to use.

Thinking like an international business manager

International business is a discipline that is crucial to companies' performance and is often dealt with on a strategic level as well as regional levels. It is important to note that there is still considerable disagreement and debate among academics and practitioners about how international business as a discipline is regarded, because many other core disciplines are also dealt with in this field. The boundaries of international business are almost unlimited, and many of those studying international business will fill positions in international business management and international business development, but also in regional business management, international project management, international marketing, international finance, and similar.

International business studies has a long history in a variety of other fields such as economics, management, sociology and political science, but as a discipline, is only fully recognized for a rather short time.

1 Much of international trade theory originates in **early economics**. But the fathers of this relatively recent discipline are, among others, Hymer (1960) with his early, economics-based study of international investments, Vernon (1994) with his product life cycle theory that you will revisit in section 2.4, in his 1960s research project into **manufacturing investment**; Dunning (1989), with his early works on ownership, location and internalization criteria for investment activities, is part of this history.

2 Dunning, in particular, then made significant contributions to the understanding of **origins** of international business and **worldwide investment movements**.

3 The Uppsala internationalization school (e.g. Johanson and Wiedersheim, 1975) significantly contributed to the development of the **stages model of internationalization**.

4 Later on, much was learned from **comparative business** studies, but this was soon neglected to the benefit of multinational enterprise studies.

5 **Transaction costs** were given attention in a theory that would be used to explain patterns of horizontal and vertical integration in natural resource and manufacturing industries, by authors such as Hennart (1991), and open the elaboration of the testing of **emerging theoretical models**.

6 Caves (1998) works on the foundation that international business's 'economic analysis enjoys a great advantage in its unified theoretical view of **market processes** and **allocative decisions**'. This is also the time when further awareness was to take shape, that of managerial capabilities as well as political, cultural and social contexts that determine international business in a **multidisciplinary** way.

7 Being more and more focalized on the study of multinational enterprises, international business research recognizes that comparative, **local knowledge** based research needs to be stimulated so that one may learn from interdisciplinary studies, enriched by an attention to **contexts** and **case studies** of firms, of sectors and of regions.

❝I define IB knowledge as an integrative field combining knowledge of core IB 'rules of the game' for IB and commerce with regional know-how, creating a unified knowledge platform that is theory based and inimitable to constituencies whose capabilities are limited to a single axis of the matrix. The general knowledge base includes knowledge of a series of fundamental tenets such as international institutions, trade agreements, regional organizations and the like. This knowledge is only partially codified, substantial and complex.❞

(Shenkar, 2004)

The key principle that all international business academics agree on is that internationalization is crucial for corporate value-adding activities, and sustains corporate growth. Also, international business management requires a high degree of adaptability and responsiveness to the great diversity of markets next to that of domestic activity.

In practice, following this principle is not always easy: international business managers have to balance the conditions they find across borders with the requirements of the headquarters. Application of objectives requires decisions about standardization or regional/local adaptation. For example, supplier agreements in China are subject to different legal requirements, cultures and socio-economic conditions than in the UK, in the USA, in Peru or in India. Each business environment is different, and the efficient international business manager strives to exploit possible similarities, and simultaneously deals with the differences. In this, one core competence is to turn diversity into value. For example, particular innovative competencies that one may find in one part of the world can feed into needs for products or services that are produced or engineered in another part of the world, (often for cost or expertise advantages) and that might be sold in yet another part of the world.

Therefore, the international business manager analyses a multitude of factors before and while managing the firm's activities across borders. Going international means, for a firm, to explore the return, i.e. the benefits that it obtains from different business environments. At the same time, it assesses the risks that are always more important than when a company only operates on a domestic level. Nonetheless, in the latter case, it will be exposed to significant competition from foreign companies and from domestic competitors that work internationally.

Also, it will still be subject to legislation that harmonizes and regulates business in its region, and that results from governmental and non-governmental convergence effects of globalization. For example, a French company that only operates and sells locally is nonetheless under the obligation to act in conformity to French and also European Union legislation, say, in labour law, environmental requirements or for product labelling, and much more. An international business manager knows how to use these differences (market imperfections) and convergence effects to the benefit of the company.

If you take only one thing away from your international business course, take this: always make sure that the diversity of business environments is used as a value!

International business practice can be considered as being all the activities that happen at the interface between the company and the international environment, i.e. non-domestic world. The field of international business changes very quickly because of its complexity and the many interactions that constitute the interface between locations, markets and the firm. International business focuses on buying, selling or exchanging commodities within a country or between countries, international trade and investments. The international business manager determines entry into the marketplaces that are the best for a given firm or product or service, and is dependent on specific information, for example through industry directories, and logistic tools help locate customers and suitable businesses and specific trade information.

The terms, place, time and conditions for internationalization, that is to say, the involvement and engagement of a firm across borders, in the short and long term, are managed by the international business manager. These are the fields that you will study in your course.

Studying international business

International business is a discipline that is best studied in an environment and with classmates that demonstrate diversity, for example, different cultures and origins. Talking with people who have different opinions, ideas and suggestions teaches you, on a small scale, to deal with international diversity, to accept that people and perspectives vary, and that acceptance, tolerance and flexibility are part of the toolkit that make you succeed in this environment. It is great fun, so make sure that you encounter many international students, and engage into discussions with them. Obviously, international travel is, wherever possible, recommended to enhance what you learned in your course. If you are an experienced traveller, do not hesitate to share your experiences with your classmates. Also, case studies and guest seminars from international managers and executives, whether from small, medium or large enterprises, illustrate the learning and help apply it later, in exams or in your career. If you have the opportunity to talk to, interview and encounter professionals in the area, you should make sure that you talk to them about your learning and ask about their application of it.

Questions to ponder

Even if your course does not culminate in an exam, it is always useful to ponder on a few questions that make you think about the material you have learned. This Companion will help you to make the information you have read applicable, in a research project, a discussion round and your future career.

If your course culminates in an exam, then the Companion helps you revise for likely exam questions.

The sections are written to be clear, short and instructive, but also raise questions and deal with topics that prepare you for any further topics, those that one finds often in exams and in discussions of classroom material that help you participate constructively in your own learning, that of your classmates, and obtain the appreciation of your examiner. To help with some of these issues, that are formulated as 'Exam questions', the writer provides some brief guidance on how you could approach the answer, but you should go further and try to fill in the detail and think of how you could set up a bit of a discussion of the matters raised. This will help you to move one step forward from just being able to recite the lists of features etc. provided in the text. But watch out for the pitfalls! This book points out some of them, so that you know what to expect.

References to more information

The textbook(s) that have been recommended on your course are your primary source of information, with this Companion as a clear and precise help for your revisions. If your course syllabus list is lengthy with recommended readings, it may be difficult to focus on essentials. Guidance is needed as to what to read. Possibly, you have access to a course handbook or a support website with the materials and the subjects covered in your lectures and seminars. There are several excellent textbooks that are frequently referred to in this Sage Course Companion and which I can thoroughly recommend. These are mainly:

- Rugman and Collinson (2006) *International Business*
- Hill (2008) *Global Business*
- Czinkota, Ronkainen and Moffett (2007) *International Business*
- Punnett and Ricks (1998) *International Business*

Full reference to these textbooks is provided in the Bibliography. More of them are listed at the end of each section where applicable and thought to be relevant for your learning.

part two

core areas of the IB curriculum

Introduction to the running themes in the book

The running themes of the book are mainly in accordance with those in the main international business textbooks. This is to help the reader to complement the instructions provided by international business lectures. Nonetheless, some liberty was taken in the addition of themes that are recent and that evolve with globalization and the never-ending evolutions of the international business environment. The objective is to help students stay at the top of the subject, and allow the sound preparation for tests, quizzes and projects that you may be asked to engage in.

This guide mainly deals with the toolkit that any future international business manager will need. We start this main part off with **International Business (IB) basics** and fundamentals. This section provides the main terminology that you need to get used to in this field, through first reflections on globalization, regionalism and the ever-changing international business environment that corporations have to continuously adapt to.

At the very basis of international business activity is the underlying belief that international trade and investment are beneficial to companies. **Trade and investment theory** explores why this is so, and explains why international business exists. This text shows how IB was increasingly well understood: like this, models and tools could be conceived that we use to know how to run successful international operations.

The very foundation of the international economy, international trade and IB is the diversity of environments that a corporation has to deal with when it works across borders. This is the theme of our review of **culture, politics and law** that have to be known and managed, and that are part of the complexity in which international business evolves.

Some countries and regions make strong efforts to regulate international business activity for the benefit of trade partners. **Economic Integration and Trade Relations** typically aim to facilitate trade and to increase the welfare of the populations, with effects on trade patterns and the possibilities to enter into and benefit from the market.

Globalization strives strongly through the internationalization of the financial sector. International business is embedded in the global **monetary system** that includes exchange rate risks and other phenomena that any international business manager is familiar with, because the firm is exposed to these.

On the basis of the knowledge acquired about the international business environment, its conditions and realities, a firm can engage in **internationalization**: functioning across borders requires the application of theory and practice, tools and human resources' (HR) strategies that help satisfy entry motivations and exert entry strategies (entry modes). An explicit, well-adapted international strategy determines how a firm operates on the foreign markets and what **organizational behaviour** is required to obtain the desired results. **Business operations** are adapted to this strategy and the organizational requirements, ranging from logistics to international marketing.

Not to be forgotten, in greater complexity and diversity, a firm will not only gain from benefits and a multitude of opportunities. It will also be exposed to **risks and uncertainties**. Indeed, increasing globalization causes economic, financial and social exchanges. At the same time, it increases the impact of business risks because risks and uncertainties are to be managed on a global scale.

Yet another main management tool in international business is that of **knowledge management**, in which units of international corporations will transfer knowledge about experiences made, ways and manners of solving issues, and make sure that the firm will not engage resources in duplication of efforts. The management tools then help monitor and optimize international business activity.

This optimization, or value creation, is situated in a political economy that preserves its local and global dimension: the international economy and trade are ruled by a large number of instances, authorities and actors. **International institutions, governmental and non-governmental organizations** are an integral part of the international business environment. They monitor, survey, incite, control, facilitate and regulate the conditions in which international business functions.

The running themes exposed here will now be examined and structured in a manner that will allow you to study them efficiently, and to facilitate comprehension of these essential issues.

Recommended reading

RUGMAN AND COLLINSON (2006)

CZINKOTA, RONKAINEN AND MOFFETT (2007)

HILL (2008)

2.1

international business basics: terminologies and first reflections on globalization, regionalism and international commerce

This companion guide starts in the same manner as the main textbooks in the field of International Business, with a two-fold preoccupation. The one is to introduce the reader to the terminology in this field of study; the other is to place the reading and guidance of this work into the modern world of contemporary business.

This book is written for corporations and their current or future managers, many of you who are sitting in classrooms, libraries, at PCs or at desks when studying from it. Of course, you already know that the business world is ever-changing, with tools that develop from the analysis of past and current practices and for future performance. This guide is a key to learning and understanding those tools.

Some concepts need definition before you start to work through these sections. The terminology of international business evolves with the phenomena of globalization that follows and drives international business.

International business is, all at the same time, about the activity of trading, investing and operating in countries other than the domestic home base, and about the companies doing this.

Globalization is a phenomenon that will often be referred to, in this framework. It is the integration of economic, social, technological, political and possibly other exchanges throughout the world, of goods, services, knowledge, and much more. Much debate is given to whether the effects of such intensive exchange are only positive or negative, and whether this phenomenon will lead to one single standardized world. In any circumstances, what we refer to here is economic international integration, also defined as the compression of time and space: globalization means that less time is needed to shift products, services or knowledge across the world, thus virtually reducing space. Geographies appear to shrink because technology, information flows and logistical tools have made markets seem closer to one another.

The phenomenon of globalization is accompanied by that of regionalism. This is another often-used term in international business studies, implying that regions, regional identities and local goods, services, customs, values and preferences have become more important to people at the same time as globalization rises too. Successful international business therefore needs to balance out local and global expectations and advantages.

The major textbooks introduce this theme with an analysis of the globalization of markets and production (for example, Hill (2008), Chapter 1).

The key concepts here are that:

- markets converge, in many ways, on a global marketplace (although this phenomenon is not complete)
- production activities can be optimized throughout the world, i.e. costs being reduced, value added, innovation enhanced, knowledge shared internationally.

Corporations mainly go international because they perform better when they benefit from these optimization effects. The firms do this in different ways, use different manners of approaching markets, of locating operations, and of structuring such internationalization. Among international firms, multinational enterprises are firms that operate in more than one foreign country, with a variety of relationships and interests abroad, and headquarters in one country. Transnational firms are yet more borderless in nature, and localize their operations, units and subsidiaries strongly, so as to adapt to different regions.

Exam question: One pertinent exam question is to advise whether a firm, in a particular sector and activity, would better function as a multinational or a transnational company. You may want to argue that, typically, consumer-oriented firms will show a tendency to operate in a less standardized, rather localized manner, i.e. as transnational firms, while firms that can easily capture markets with standardized products will rather function as multinationals.

Among those international firms, both small- and medium-sized enterprises (SME) and large enterprises (LEs) are represented. For example, in Europe, SMEs constitute more than three-quarters of all companies. More and more start-ups are 'born globals', which means that their supplies, functions, markets and operations are international from the very beginning onwards. Other corporations prefer to internationalize through a steady expansion of interests and equity across borders.

International trade strongly sustains international business, because international trade is based on the relations between countries that exchange goods or services, and will hopefully do so in reciprocity, i.e. on similar terms for mutual benefit. You will learn later that the political economy is of fundamental importance in international business, across countries and physical (and increasingly, virtual) environments.

International business targets a diversity of locations and spaces, with different business conditions and environments. These concern natural, human, cultural, social, economic and much other specificity of regions and areas around the world that an international firm may need and use for productions, operations or as markets. This influences the manner in which international business is conducted. Among these specificities, geological features determine what resources a firm may be able to count with. Also, considerations ranging from the fertility of grounds to infrastructures and the possibilities for the transport of goods or delivery of services determine business opportunities. Water, soil and commodities such as gas and oil, define opportunities (e.g. for production) and responsibilities (e.g. for the environment). Weather conditions affect particular business sectors and also ways of doing business.

Human conditions also affect international business, in particular:

- population: number, education, skills, culture, social conditions, migration
- economics and politics: stability, growth, infrastructure, among others.

The interaction of such factors, as Czinkota et al. (2007) note, change over time. Internationally active firms have to adapt to such change and use their knowledge in accordance with these conditions. This adds on to the complexity of international business, but can be of great competitive advantage vis-à-vis domestic firms.

An increasingly virtual dimension of international business is enhanced by widespread, easily accessible and effective use of technology around the world. Few of the major international business textbooks go into detail about these issues, but one reads about them, experiences them in the workplace and, as a student, learns about them through case studies. Students can download their courses from wherever they may be located, can follow e-learning modules and use podcasts to stimulate efficient learning. In a similar way, companies use the internet and ICT (Information and Communication Technology) tools to reach partners and markets across the world. Also, firms are increasingly exposed to the fast and pitiless comments and opinions that travel around the world on blogs, forums and other tools and on which people judge the performance, ethics and image of the companies. Companies that function across borders, in whatever manner it may be, operate in more complex business environments, because there are many different places around the world with a great diversity of stakeholders, i.e. parties related to the business activities, closely or from far, may be influenced by it and may have some impact on it. This includes not only suppliers, purchasers, distributors, trade unions, economic partners and consumers, but also governmental authorities, institutions, organizations, infrastructures, and people living in the communities in which goods are produced, resources are extracted and utilized, and products or services are proposed. This opens us up to challenges and opportunities.

The further you progress in your study of international business, the more you are required to use critical thinking and to think further about the way in which companies react to changes in an international business environment that is complex, ever-changing and requires flexibility and adaptation skills. A great manager and leader in international business needs foremost a great responsiveness to change, and a will to learn continuously.

Because international business is that far-reaching in scale and in scope, some issues become important over time and across borders. For example, does international business know, manage and adapt to climate change? Does international business play a role in politics and geopolitics? How ethically does a firm behave in other countries? How does its management respond to corruption?

 Taking it **FURTHER**

Transparency International, founded in 1993, is one of the organizations that trace trade partners' and business' behaviours in the field of corruption. It mainly uses awareness-raising campaigns (reports, indexes, handbooks) and research studies to diminish tolerance of visible or less visible corruption, and hence aims also to hinder the distortion of international trade.

" Corruption is the abuse of entrusted power for private gain. It hurts everyone whose life, livelihood or happiness depends on the integrity of people in a position of authority. "

> (Transparency International (2007) Global Corruption Report and Transparency International Malaysia Report www.transparency.org/)

The adoption of fair trade principles – through a social movement, fair trade promotes fair prices, ethics and increasing responsibilities in international trade. In particular, trade between developing and developed countries is targeted here. Fair trade helps vulnerable communities attain self-sufficiency, and to not be exposed to the power of wealthy companies. At the same time, its critics argue that floor prices (minimum amounts payable to the local producers) distort prices because they are typically above market prices, and may lead to an artificial and abundant supply level. Fair trade therefore needs to be responsive to markets, with international buyers willing to purchase, and needs to be accompanied by complementary initiatives such as diversification and the preservation of identities of cultures and their produce. Fair trade is an example of the way in which companies can also adjust to trends and requirements in the international business environment. Some firms have dedicated their product range entirely to fair trade, while maximizing profits and creating value for their shareholders (i.e. owners of stock, expecting a return on their investment) at the same time. Such trends in international business are studied by think tanks and consulting firms.

McKinsey's Global Survey points out the rising impact of consumers in emerging countries in the coming years. UNIDO (United Nations Industrial Development Organization) explores the impact of outsourcing trends, while the World Economic Forum stresses the rising importance of security and crisis management in the future. OECD (Organisation for Economic Co-Operation and Development) publishes international investment perspectives, similar to those of IMF (International Monetary Fund). Corporations adapt to changing customer expectations and adopt related business models – for example, based on 'free' products or services that are financed through advertising or other indirect tools, such as through AdWords and cookies at Google Inc. International business optimizes its performance through the benefits of diversity in trade.

Recommended reading

RUGMAN AND COLLINSON (2006)
CZINKOTA ET AL. (2007)
HILL (2008)

2.2

international trade and investment theory

The leading International Business textbooks either start out on a basis of trade and investment theory, or else come to it within the body of the book at various points. It therefore makes sense to review the main concepts and theories at this early stage. It will give you a sound basis for your international business studies and you will be more likely to provide well-founded responses in the assignments and exercises that you will come across in all following sub-fields.

International trade and investment theory is an essential underpinning of all concepts that you will study in International Business (IB). A great many students resent theory as something 'dry' and uninteresting: in the field of IB, you will find that examples of these theories surround us everyday and everywhere, so they are likely to arouse your interest. Also, thinking of how you are influenced by IB will help you answer exam questions more easily – for example: where does your laptop come from? Where does the brand originate from? Where are the components made? Where did you buy it; where do you use it? Why is that so?

International trade is all about exchanging goods and services among foreign economies. It has become an important topic because most economies have changed from a state-driven to a market-driven economic system throughout the past decades. Trade with some economies (countries and regions) in the world is booming, while other economies appear to be less concerned. This is due to the resources and conditions that are sought by engaging in international trade.

International trade is a complex machinery that links trade, economics, management and public policy issues, among others. It influences the national economic indicators of a nation's wealth such as unemployment or inflation. As a consequence, many economists, starting with Adam Smith, the 'father' of economics, have tried to explain the relationship between free trade and economic wealth.

International trade and investment theory helps you to:

- understand the traditional arguments of how and why international trade improves the welfare of all countries: why not only trade domestically?
- use history as a basis to learn from, and compare the implications of trade theory from the original work of Adam Smith to the contemporary theories of Michael Porter and further
- examine the criticisms of classical trade theory and examine alternative viewpoints of which business and economic forces determine trade policy between countries, as well as international management decisions
- explore why trade and investment are different and engage economies and business leaders in various evolving strategies.

Trade policies are designed by governments to regulate, direct, and protect national economic activity and welfare. On the basis of national sovereignty, a government exercises the right to shape the environment of the country and its citizens. The main objectives of governmental authorities are to increase their citizens' living standards, improve the quality of life, and to achieve high employment rates. Governmental authorities hence shape the environment in which corporations exercise trade and run investments.

Taking it *FURTHER*

In democratic countries, governmental authorities' interest in economic growth and welfare is stirred by the desire of re-election and mainly maintained through a civil service administration that keeps a long-term focus on its objectives.

If international trade exists nevertheless, there must be good reasons for it that counterbalance or complement the apparent simplicity and advantages of domestic trade. No one single theory explains these factors on its own. Because IB is more complex than domestic trade and has evolved significantly over time, each theory has its own merit and complements earlier findings.

Remember the absolute 'must knows':

- The age of Mercantilism
- Classical Trade Theory: Smith and Ricardo
- Factor Proportions Theory
- International Investment and Product Cycle Theory
- The New Trade Theory: Strategic Trade
- The Theory of International Investment

Mercantilism: 16th to 18th centuries

Mercantilism has given one of the first clues to the interrogation of why nations trade with one another, at a time when gold was the world currency (18th century). European nations suggested that their wealth would be accelerated when exports were encouraged and imports stifled in order to reach a *positive trade balance*. The currency would hence flow into the economy. As a consequence, it was argued that the more gold that was accumulated in the country, the more powerful it was to be.

Mercantilism does not focus on specialization but concentrates on policy. Some economies, such as the French nationalizations in the 1970s/80s, and China in the early 2000s, showed a trend towards mercantilist policies.

The Theory of Absolute Advantage: Adam Smith

The theory of *absolute advantage* is the starting point for an explanation of international trade through the specialization lens. It was developed by Adam Smith, a Scottish economist, philosopher and author of *The Wealth of Nations* (1776).

By specializing in the production of goods that an economy can produce more efficiently than any other, he stated, nations can increase their economic well-being.

The productivity approach is the key factor in economic development. Country X has an absolute advantage over Country Y when it is able to produce the same good faster, better; cheaper (we only speak of efficient production here). Countries will export the goods produced with the lowest labour-hours needed. Country X which has an absolute advantage on certain goods will have to export those goods and import the goods that it is lacking. Country Y holds the absolute advantage for another good. The two countries will engage into trade relations to a mutual benefit.

Following this theory, one can assume that countries try to maximise the use of their natural resources in order to manufacture the same products with fewer labour-hours than competitors in other countries. But, in order to be efficient, the production process must be performed exclusively by one individual actor in each stage. It creates a division of labour. Each country specializes in one product (or service, if we extend this theory) for which it is uniquely suitable. With his works, Adam Smith hence advocated free trade and pioneered modern economics.

At that time, the value of a product was determined by its use or by what it could acquire in exchange, both of which were inconsistent standards of measurement, according to Smith. Instead, he argued that value should depend on another factor.

" Labour was the first price, the original purchase – money that was paid for all things. It was not by gold or by silver, but by labour, that all wealth of the world was originally purchased. "

(*The Wealth of Nations*, Adam Smith, 1776)

For Smith, this factor was mainly that of labour, in the early stages of socio-economic evolution. At the same time, he explored concepts of self-interest and its role in the economy, the division of labour, the function of markets, and the international implications of a *laissez-faire* economy.

Following Adam Smith's work, self-interest appeared to stimulate the efficient use of resources in a nation's economy (the Invisible Hand), of public welfare as a by-product, and of market forces.

" It is not from the benevolence of the butcher, the brewer, or the baker that we expect our dinner, but from their regard to their own interest. "

(*The Wealth of Nations*, Adam Smith, 1776)

Remember that as a main merit, this theory stipulates that gains from international trade can be created. These gains can be enhanced through further specialization, but cannot be evenly distributed in the domestic economy because not all actors specialize in the relevant good and production.

The labour theory of value prevailed among classical economists in the mid-19th century. It mainly found its expression in Marxian economics. Today, the theory of marginal utility replaces it: a good or service holds its utility (use) in its least urgent use of the most desired available uses, i.e. the use that is right in the margin that may vary for individuals and companies.

The Theory of Comparative Advantage: David Ricardo

The Theory of Comparative Advantage demonstrates that gains from international trade also persist when both countries excel in the production of two of the same goods, and trade with each other. David Ricardo, an English-born economist sparked by the reading of Smith's *Wealth of Nations*, worked upon the concept of the division of labour and its equilibrium through the mechanism of relative prices. The theory, elaborated in the early 19th century, holds that nations should produce the goods excelling through the greatest *relative* advantage.

In the example of Portugal and England and two commodities (wine and cloth), trade was to be beneficial even if Portugal held an absolute cost advantage over England in both wine and cloth. Because each economy specializes in the production of the good in which it has a comparative cost advantage and trades with the other nation for the other good, both nations are able to benefit from the exchange. Ricardo argued at the same time that factors, particularly labour, are not mobile across borders. Economic growth and wealth are increased if goods (excluding luxuries) are imported at a lower price than they cost domestically. Overall income levels would rise in both nations because domestic industry can concentrate on more advantageous goods, according to factor advantages, creating efficiencies, providing labour and increasing purchasing powers.

According to Ricardo's theory, countries trade on a win–win basis, exchanging their specialized production. That is the consequence of differences between production techniques, capital and labour and productivity.

For olive oil (100 litres) and pasta (50 kg), Spain may need respectively one and three hours for production, while Italy may use five and seven hours. According to Adam Smith, Spain has an absolute advantage over Italy regarding olive oil and pasta production since it manufactures both products within fewer hours than Italy. As a consequence, one can understand why Spain will export olive oil and pasta to Italy. Using Ricardo's theory, Spain owns a larger relative advantage (1/5) regarding olive oil production than pasta production (3/7). In this case, one can understand that Spain will produce and export olive oil. Italy, with a larger relative advantage in pasta production (7/3) than olive oil (5/1) will produce and export pasta.

Extensions of Ricardo's work: Karl Marx

Some main contributions and extensions of Ricardo's work were made by John Stuart Mill (1848) and Karl Marx (1867–94). The latter, among his works, confirmed the relation established by Ricardo between labour and value; for Marx, the value of a product is based on the **labour** used for its **production** (a variable capital) and **capital** (as a constant capital). The value of a commodity is the socially necessary labour time embodied.

Another extension: The Theory of the International Values – John Stuart Mill

John Stuart Mill, a liberal British philosopher and economist of the 19th century, advocated, among others, the use of economic theory in political decision-making. In this theory of international values, Mill clarifies the mechanisms for fixing the terms for exchanges. He explains that when products of one country are exchanged with products of another, the value of the exports should be equal to the value of the imports. This work was hence exploring the law of international values in terms of reciprocal demands of countries for each other's products.

The Theory of Factor Proportions: Eli Heckscher and Bertil Ohlin

In 1933, the Swedish academics Heckscher and Ohlin explain international trade by the abundance or rarity of factors of production. They in particular expand the number of factors of production to two, i.e. labour and capital, and explore the variations of these factors across industries, economies and international trade, in their ratio.

Remember Heckscher and Ohlin for their model that relates two factors of production: 'labour' and 'capital'.

The two economists considered that different goods required different proportions of these two factors of production. The price of these factors then determines cost differences and these prices are determined by the endowments of labour and capital the country has. The Factor Proportions Theory argues for a country to specialize in the production and export of those products for which it uses intensively its relatively abundant factor. This implies that a relatively capital abundant country must ideally specialize in the production of capital-intensive goods and should export these goods in exchange for labour-intensive goods that would come from a relatively labour-abundant country. One important condition here is that the markets for the inputs and the outputs are perfectly competitive. The theory holds only when both countries use identical technologies, while the earlier Ricardian model assumed that production technologies differ.

Pitfall

Watch out for a typical question that you may be asked in class and that goes as follows (or similar): If China excels in leather footwear manufacturing and the USA in computer memory chips, how should the two countries specialize in production in accordance with these goods? With the Heckscher–Ohlin model, you are well-advised to argue that the manufacturing of leather footwear is still a relatively labour-intensive process, even with the most sophisticated leather treatment. Other goods, such as computer memory chips, although requiring some highly skilled labour, require massive quantities of capital for production.

The H-O model, later extended by Samuelson and Vanek, among others, shows that international trade will occur, as nationally advantageous. It has quantifiable effects upon prices, wages and rents, because of relative factor endowment differences between trading nations, and when different industries use factors in varying proportions.

❝ ... there have been many theories regarding international trade from Smith to now. Each of these theories has turned to be a starting point for more understanding. For instance, Ricardo's comparative advantage is the evolution of Smith's absolute advantage theory, the following Leontief's paradox is an evolution of Heckcher and Ohlin theory ... Each time we realise that a theory cannot really apply entirely to the real world, another theory is needed. ❞

('Funeral by funeral, theory advances'. Paul Samuelson)

The Leontief paradox: Wassily Leontief

Leontief, an American economist of Russian origin, and Nobel Prize winner for economic sciences in 1973, established the famous Leontief paradox. He was particularly known for his work in qualitative economics, through input–output analysis. Based on the theory of factor proportions, Leontief studied American trade and expected exports of strongly capitalized products and imports of products that required a large amount of labour. By his study in 1947–53, he had put in evidence of the specialization of the USA in labour-intensive products instead of capital-intensive ones, which was surprising. It counters the theory of factor proportions. With this, Leontief showed the importance of clarifying the quality of the factors of production by taking into consideration the particular characteristics of each co-exchanger's countries.

The H-O theory predicted that countries would export the products that use their abundant factors intensively. In 1947, Wassily Leontief tested whether the factor proportions theory could be used to explain the types of goods the USA imported and exported.

Leontief's contribution to international trade is the understanding that one theory alone cannot explain the phenomenon and that one needs to complement the factor proportions theory of international trade.

The Product Life Cycle Theory: Raymond Vernon

The American economist R. Vernon shed light on international trade mechanisms with a focus on the cycle of life of a product. It helped explain how and at what stage firms move their products and innovations through international markets. Studying the nature of innovation in the USA and firm strategy for the product in question, he observed four phases in a product's life cycle:

- Stage 1: *the new product*. The product requires highly skilled labour and large quantities of capital for research and development. It is only a prototype (meaning non-standardized) and is extremely expensive. The product is made and sold only in the innovative country.
- Stage 2: *the maturing product*. The product becomes standardized, all the production fees decline, economies of scale are made, and the product is exported to other developed, high-income countries.
- Stage 3: *the standardized product*. The mature product. It is being bought by all kinds of populations and the market is saturated. There is development of ranges around the product.
- Stage 4: *the decline*. The product becomes obsolete and its technology is old-fashioned. There is less interest in the product.

An oft-cited, pertinent example of this theory is the product life cycle of photocopiers. Photocopiers were developed in the early 1960s by Xerox in the USA. At first, Xerox exported photocopiers from the USA to other advanced countries. As demand began to grow in these countries, Xerox entered into joint ventures to set up production in Japan, called Fuji-Xerox, and Great Britain, called Rank-Xerox. Once Xerox's patents expired, other foreign competitors began to enter the market. As a consequence, exports from the USA declined, and users began to buy photocopiers from lower-cost foreign sources, such as from Japan. More recently, Japanese companies found that their own country was too expensive to manufacture photocopiers, so they began to switch production to developing countries such as Singapore and Thailand, and to add more innovation.

Economies of Scale, the New Trade Theory and Network Theory

In the 1970s and the 1980s, the New Trade Theory challenges and extends classical economic models for international trade. You will study extensions of international trade theory that were made ever since, by, among others, the American economist Paul Krugman. He suggested in the 1990s that trade reflects an overlay of increasing-returns specialization on comparative advantage in the frame of *monopolistic competition*. Formerly, increasing returns were only thought to alter the pattern of comparative advantage. Important firms are recognized as being able to obtain great scale benefits and low cost per unit, called *Economies of Scale*; thus a firm holding international economies of scale can potentially monopolize an industry and create an imperfect market. According to Krugman, a firm should produce the volume necessary for economies of scale – cost benefits and other firms in other countries may produce products that are similar in order to exchange them. Similar products are then substitutable for the consumer, with the same process of production for the producer. Staffan Burenstam Linder's Overlapping Product Ranges Theory explained that trade in manufactured goods is dictated by similarities in product demands across countries, not by cost concerns. He introduced the network effects of consumption (resulting in market segments).

" Globalization, like the telephone, is both a blessing and a curse ... Globalization is like a giant wave that can either capsize nations or carry them forward on its crest ... "

" ... Yet, only 30 countries share 56% of the world GDP and 72% of trade flows. This implies that only a minority of countries take advantage of the Smithonian and Ricardian trade aspirations. Today, the large majority of countries do not take part in the gains of international trade. **"**

(Joseph E. Stiglitz)

Michael Porter's Diamond

Harvard Professor Michael Porter specialized in competitive strategy and the competitiveness of economic development, examined the competitiveness of industries on a global basis and contributed the so-called *Diamond of National Advantage* to our understanding of international trade. In this model, in diamond shape, innovation is what drives and sustains competitiveness. Four components define competition that are factor conditions, demand conditions, related and supporting industries, and firm strategy, structure, and rivalry. Knowing and mastering these forces helps the firm to obtain or maintain its competitive advantage through an adapted *value chain*. Porter adds that Competitive Clusters create a critical mass of unexpected competitive success in specific fields, located in one place based on public–private initiatives.

The Theory of International Investment

This theory, developed through the recognition of globalizations' effects upon firm behaviour that exceed simple trade relations (exports and imports), illustrates that the movement of capital has allowed foreign direct investments across the globe. Firms have evolved into 'seekers', seeking resources, factor advantages, knowledge, security and markets. Also, firms are seen as exploiters of imperfections in access, factor mobility, management, and internalizers that establish their own multinational operations and internalize production.

Note: The firms' competitive advantage is hence strongly dependent on confidentiality.

Indeed, the classical theories were thought to be insufficient to explain modern globalization effects, economies of scale, currency crises, network effects, with the perfect competition less realistic than, for example, the assumptions made by *monopolistic competition*. When a monopolistically competitive market expands, a mixture of more firms (greater product variety) and bigger firms drives with bigger scale economies. Liberal trade hence expands market size across borders, to the benefit of firms and consumers.

Recommended reading

RUGMAN AND COLLINSON (2006), *Chapter 6*
CZINKOTA ET AL. (2007), *Chapter 5*
PUNNETT AND RICKS (1998), *Chapter 3*
HILL (2008), *Chapter 4*

2.3

foundations of international economy and trade: culture, politics, law and ethics

The significance of culture in IB

In international business, culture is not, as often would be as first thought, defined as it is in civil life, in which you will think of museums, concerts, churches. These are elements of culture, in fact, expressions of it. You will become familiar with culture as:

❝the acquired knowledge that people use to interpret experience and to generate social behaviour.❞

(James Spradley)

❝Culture is the collective programming of the human mind that distinguishes the members of one human group from those of another. Culture in this sense is a system of collectively held values.❞

(Geert Hofstede)

" Culture is the deeper level of basic assumptions and beliefs that are shared by members of an organization, that operate unconsciously and define in a basic 'taken for granted' fashion an organization's view of its self and its environment. "

(Edgar Schein)

Culture is hence the manner in which groups tend to differentiate themselves from one another, also referred to as the in- and the out-group, defined by the shared evolved knowledge of this group, defining behaviors, possessions, manners, beliefs, and communicating these amongst each other. It determines the way in which we see matters as right or wrong, normal or strange, valuable or worthless.

These cultures can be seen within nations, organizations, religions, professions, sectors and industries, and many other determined groups that conceive of a certain way of doing and thinking as the most relevant in the given scenario, relative to other groups.

Culture is most easily observed on the:

- national level: the nation in its collectivism, possibly with sub-groups
- regional level: ethnic, linguistic, or religious differences in a region
- gender level: gender differences (female vs. male)
- generation level: differences between grandparents and parents, parents and children, the older and younger workforce
- social class level: educational opportunities and differences in occupation, wealth and education
- corporate level: the *corporate culture* of an organization, industry or sector culture, or profession.

Taking it **FURTHER**

An estimated 53 million people globally work for companies foreign to their original culture. This globalization effect leads us to the need for understanding of how people's preferences, beliefs and values differ. Why should we? Because if one is not aware of these differences, the organization will be most likely to fail in international marketing efforts, internationalization strategies, international negotiations, merger and acquisitions, and simply making multiculturalism a positive value.

Working with different cultures is part of the day-to-day realities of international business. In the best case, multiculturalism becomes a value and a comparative advantage. In the worst case, however, cross-cultural miscomprehensions hinder business opportunities through *ethnocentrism*, i.e. one believes one's culture to be superior to others.

> *Some lecturers teach multicultural issues limiting the focus upon human resources and negotiations. Others go further, and add processes and methodologies that move from 'looking at the differences' to 'creating value'. The latter will also examine the international subsidiary management, for example, and organization, leadership and communication. One quiz question may ask about the need for autonomy or control of subsidiaries in different cultures.*

Weaknesses and failures in communication are part of the most apparent problems in multicultural management. In the company-to-company context, contracts, alliances, joint ventures and mergers and acquisitions can fail or become complicated if cultural aspects have not been taken into consideration.

> Consider the cultural difficulties of Pharmacia and Upjohn, or Daimler Chrysler. In the customer relation, the different consumer preferences, cultures and habits require adaptations. They may result in costs but can open new markets and specialization. Some leading international corporations (such as Ford, Palmolive and Parker Pen) encountered some marketing mistakes in advertising campaigns, and had to learn the hard way. These mistakes are always due to a lack of knowledge about cultural difference or *ethnocentrism*. They result in significant inefficiencies.

" Culture is more often a source of conflict than of synergy. Cultural differences are a nuisance at best and often a disaster. "

(Hofstede)

" Misunderstanding of national cultural differences have been cited as the most important factors behind the high failure rate of global JVs and alliances. "

(Piero Morosini, author of *Managing Cultural Differences*, 2003)

Business negotiations are often used to illustrate cultural difference. A negotiation in Western countries will aim for mutual agreement and handshakes when that agreement is reached, i.e. the end of negotiations starting a partnership of some sort. In Middle Eastern countries, agreement leads to handshaking, indicating that now further details can be explored through further negotiation. Germans and North-Americans prefer the paper-based agreements while Spaniards and Italians will be satisfied with the verbal promise.

Pitfall

In Multiple Choice Questions (MCQ), it is important to remember your professor's culture. It is rather common to see students misinterpret potential answers because they read with their own cultural background in mind. Never hesitate to ask for help on terms that could be misunderstood.

In any structure, knowledge and work, the collection and the spread of information, the measurement of results, and the creation of forecasts rely on an efficient organizational structure. A multinational needs to be well adapted to the cultural specificities of each region, i.e. the way in which management, delegation, personnel and human resource issues and operational issues are most efficiently implemented.

The different types of business are organized:

- along their *corporate culture*, or
- along that of their owners or
- along that of the headquarters,

on a local as well as a global level.

For **example**, a family business is normally rather organic, directive and individually oriented, while entrepreneurial businesses tend to be unsystematic and group-focused. Professional service firms (for example, consulting companies) have an individualist focus and are mechanistic, but they

(Continued)

> *(Continued)*
>
> can also be group-oriented. MNEs are mainly characterized as mechanistic and autocratic. Leadership styles and leaders' performance are culturally determined. Leadership differs among managers of different cultures; its acceptance is defined by the convergence with employees' own culture.

The better you understand the verbal and non-verbal communication tools of the corporate leader, the better you can understand the message, share it, feel close to it and engage in the objectives that need to be reached.

Theories of cultural dimensions

Different theorists have defined a variety of dimensions to understand cultures. The table below summarizes three of them, which are analysed in all major IB books.

'It's good to know what to look out for, if I want to understand other cultures. But how can I help my company adapt better, and make a value out of differences?'

The main tools taught to counteract culture clashes are:

1 awareness of the cultural differences in the company's environment and structure

2 adaptation (training programmes, job rotation, expatriation)

3 leverage of the diversity of cultures (*corporate culture* makes diversity a value).

The more complex the organization gets, the more the company needs to focus on these tools.
   This is the case:

- in any new internationalization phase
- in particular, in the creation of a joint-venture, a merger or an acquisition taking place.

Table 2.1   Useful cross-cultural management dimensions

Theorist name	Hofstede (p. 134 in Rugman)	Trompenaars (p. 135)	GLOBE (p. 137)
Number of cultural dimensions	4	7	9
Dimensions	1) *power distance* (acceptance of power between instances)	1) universalism vs. particularism	1) assertiveness
	2) uncertainty avoidance	2) individualism vs. collectivism	2) future orientation
	3) individualism	3) neutral vs. emotional	3) gender differentiation
	4) masculinity	4) specific vs. diffuse	4) uncertainty avoidance
		5) achievement vs. ascription	5) *power distance*
		6) sequential vs. synchronic	6) institutional collectivism
		7) internal vs. external	7) in group/family collectivism
			8) performance orientation
			9) humane orientation

The significance of politics in IB

The economic system in which companies operate is determined by the political structure of the country.

'What is this: the political economy?'

A study of political economy examines the way in which political factors influence the functioning of economic systems.

The study of political risk, which we will refer to once again in section 2.9, examines the probability in which politics may be, now and in the future, disadvantageous to business objectives.

Hill compares two dimensions: one, the emphasis of individualism or collectivism of a government, and two, the tendency towards democracy or totalitarianism.

Democracies tend to promote **market-driven** economies (e.g. the USA) while totalitarian regimes are often characterized by a **centrally determined** market structure (e.g. the former USSR), as a command or state-directed economy.

*In your exam, do remember nonetheless that nowadays, most economies include aspects of both economic structures and are therefore **mixed** economies.*

A typical exam question: Is a democratic system essential for sustained economic development? You may want to answer this with an analysis of political vs. economic systems, with examples, and point out the pros and cons of these systems (for example, stability but lack of competitive forces in command economy; high degrees of liberalism in market economies), before you come to your conclusion.

There are essentially two ways in which the political authorities interact with business:

1. through **privatization** or **nationalization**, government **control** of assets, embargoes and sanctions, export controls, and the regulation of International Business behaviour

2. through **government–business cooperation**, trade and industrial policy, support and assistance.

Privatization can happen in the form of *contract management* (the government keeps ownership of assets but gives operational responsibility to the private company) or *divestiture* (selling of assets). The latter option is the more common one.

'Do governments typically interfere in import or export activities?'

When speaking about government–business cooperation, we should keep in mind that in many cases they refer to governmental support in high-technology R&D. In the same way, cooperation between public research institutes and companies is part of this. In international affairs, countries may establish trade barriers to protect home industry and boost cross-border trade of its own firms, to raise revenue for the government.

- These barriers mainly take the shape of *tariffs* (a tax levied on imports) or *quotas* (limiting supply from foreign producers)
- other forms of protection or obstacles to trade in national laws may concern health or packaging requirements, and language translations on packages
- also, *voluntary export restraints* (VERs) can be obtained when importers fear restrictions. The importer here proposes or agrees to limit shipping to a specific country (or regions, e.g. the EU) – this is self-imposed and not taking the shape of tariffs or quotas that are imposed by the governmental authority.

Another main part of the teaching of politics for international business is that of economic integration. We will review this in more detail in a section on its own (2.4), for its importance in regard to trade relations. Nonetheless, be aware of two different effects of integration, i.e. trade creation and trade diversion that is created through politics:

- *Trade creation* is the beneficial result of companies trading more extensively with each other within the trade union (remember the theory of comparative advantage!).
- *Trade diversion* describes the reduction of trade with companies outside the union (similar to barriers of trade, i.e. policy or regulation that restricts international trade – see above!).

Taking it **FURTHER**

Economic integration enhances international trade only if:

trade creation > trade diversion

Two important cost-reducing effects on companies operating in an integrated economic environment shouldn't be forgotten. Companies benefit from internal and external economies of scale.

- **Internal economies of scale** means that companies are able to produce at lower unit costs in larger numbers as they have to supply a bigger market; in particular, services and networks allow for strong network economies of scale.

- **External economies of scale** implies that companies have access to lower unit costs as a result of the industry growing in size.

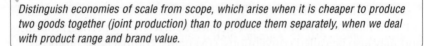

Distinguish economies of scale from scope, which arise when it is cheaper to produce two goods together (joint production) than to produce them separately, when we deal with product range and brand value.

The significance of law to IB

'Why is it important for a manager to know about international law?'

Some IB books cover law barely or not at all (Rugman et al., 2006), while others deal with this topic in great detail, making a point that corporations need not only be familiar with different legal obligations, but are subject to them.

This being said, globalization causes a great boom in corporate law, in particular for merger and acquisitions activity. Indeed, many law firms have recently merged on an international scale, and deal with IB corporate law and international law all over the world. The challenge is to bridge differences in culture, mentality, business and legal practices.

First, one has to distinguish *common law* from *civil law*.

- In regions in which *common law* is applied, courts make law as they decide individual cases. Judges in a common law jurisdiction have the power to interpret the law.
- *Civil law* originates from historical writings, was defined by kings, princes, or legislatures issuing decrees or passing bills. Judges in a civil law jurisdiction have the power only to apply the law.

 Taking it **FURTHER**

On an international level, various organizations work towards worldwide legal standards: the Incoterms of the International Chamber of Commerce (explained in section 2.8), The UN Commission on International Trade Law, The International Institute for the Unification of Private Law, and The Hague-Vishy Rules on Bills of Lading sponsored by the International Law Association are crucial parts of this.

International law in general can be divided into two types:

- Public International Law includes legal relations between governments, including all matters involving the rights and obligations of sovereign nations.
- Private International Law includes laws governing the transaction of individuals and companies crossing international borders.

Sources of this international law are bilateral and multilateral treaties between nations. Treaties are here defined as agreements between countries and may also be called conventions, covenants, compacts, or protocols.

'What kind of institution can help standardize legal obligations, for example when it comes to a firm's international contracts?'

The United Nations, for example, propose solutions that many countries, among them the USA, are ratified to apply, in the shape of the UN Convention on Contracts for International Sales of Goods. The law applicable to contracts between EU residents is determined by an amendment to the Rome Convention, which came into effect in 1991.

In a company or corporation liability issue, business divisions are divided into shares , i.e. stocks. The limited liability company holds that a liability in law of each shareholder to the company's creditors is limited to the amount to which the shareholder has agreed to invest in the company (i.e. to the value of the shares held). In the USA, for companies' partnerships, one needs to be familiar with the Partnership Act 1890. This legal text states that, in a relationship between persons carrying on business in common with a view of profit, all persons are equally liable (with the exception of Act 1970 on general/limited partners).

Taking it **FURTHER**

Most legal texts differ from one country to another. For example, you will learn that major differences in legal procedures exist in product liability. In the USA, product liability cases are heard by juries that award plaintiffs actual damages plus punitive damages. Outside the USA, product liability cases are most often heard by judges, not juries.

'But what is product liability?'

It means that a company and its officers and directors are held liable and are possibly subject to fines or imprisonment when their product causes death, injury, or damage. Strict Liability holds the designer/manufacturer liable for damages caused by a product without the need for a plaintiff to prove negligence in the product's design or manufacture.

Let us distinguish between different crucial parts of law (non-exhaustive here) that IB needs to have expertise in:

- Business law: the company is a creature of law and legitimate and socially responsible activities. Legal constraints translate societies' attempts to influence business to meet social or other issues, to observe anti-trust laws, child labour laws, equality laws, pollution-control, and/or legislation. Court decisions are precedents for the action of companies.
- Labour law: its goal is to equalize the bargaining power between employers and employees. Labour law deals with the relationship between employers and unions, and grants employees rights, in particular the right to unionize. It prohibits/allows employers and employees to engage in certain activities for their demands (e.g. strikes).
- Employment law: the individual legal relationship between employee and employer is subject to employment law. Collective bargaining agreements are key here. Legal sources are civil rights acts, fair labour standards acts, social security, disability, medical leave and worker compensation or retirement statutes.
- Intellectual Property Rights regulate and protect copyright, trade marks and patents, in the interests of the creator of materials such as authors, computer programmers, composers, artists, inventors and designers.

'Does business necessarily have to go to court to solve legal quarrels?'

In legal issues on an international level, many parties prefer arbitration (less formal, private solutions) to litigation (going to court). Sometimes they do not want or wish to accept UN or EU solutions, or do not wish to handle the cost and exposure of going to court in any country.

The International Court of Arbitration of the International Chamber of Commerce in Paris is the best known for arbitration.

People and businesses prefer arbitration for several reasons, mainly suspicion of foreign courts, speed of decision-making, informality of procedures, confidentiality, and avoidance of unwelcome publicity accompanying an open court case.

Taking it *FURTHER*

> Current and future challenges in the legal business environment of firms will focus on the regulation of commercial transactions over the internet, signature/authentication procedures, encryption and security, electronic money and copyright issues. Also, issues of corruption, ethics and social responsibility will need to be dealt with internationally.

'To what degree is the international firm under the obligation of good corporate citizenship and of acting ethically?'

Ethics in IB

"At this moment, America's highest economic need is higher ethical standards – standards enforced by strict laws and upheld by responsible business leaders."

(George W. Bush, President of the USA)

The understanding and importance of ethics is subject to cultural differences. However, firms should be familiar with common values and know what to avoid in their practices. The civil society is a group of individuals, organizations, and institutions that act outside the government and the market to advance a diverse set of interests, including opposition to global business.

Companies' citizenship is increasingly scrutinized by the **civil society** (groups acting outside government → *non-governmental organizations (NGOs)*). The civil society is part of a company's stakeholders, i.e. the community of actors concerned by corporate activities. The so-called 'stakeholder model' holds that a firm needs to satisfy not only shareholder expectations ('shareholder model', focused on profit maximization) but also those of the larger community. NGOs have obtained considerable power in influencing the public perception of MNEs. Good ethical behaviour includes the respect of human rights, adequate labour and environmental standards, fair trade, transparency and contributions to the resolve of contemporary (and evolving) global challenges (e.g. global warming, poverty, terrorism and warfare).

Moral principles are also to rule the managers' decision-making in the case of conflict within the company. The international manager has to adapt to the complex cultural and religious nuances of ethical systems, for example when dealing with conflict between subsidiaries. These decisions are considered ethical when acceptable to the moral or legal norms of the larger community, or the society.

Issues in ethics span from quality control, to abuse of sick days, to cheating on any stakeholder, price fixing or anti-competitive behaviours, discrimination, or fraud, and much more. In **exams**, you will often be asked to solve case problems that deal with questions of accountability as a solution to unethical conduct.

An increasingly strong attention is given to Corporate Social Responsibility (CSR), that is ranked by organizations such as the Dow Jones Sustainability Index, and increasingly taken into account by investors and other stakeholders of international companies. The most frequently used term is that of Corporate Social Responsibility (CSR) followed by Corporate Citizenship (CC), Strategic Philanthropy, Corporate Philanthropy and Cause-related Marketing. Corporate Social Responsibility (CSR) is defined as '... the adoption by a business of a strategic focus for fulfilling the economic, legal, ethical, and philanthropic responsibilities expected of it by its stakeholders.' (McAllister et al., 2005, p. 4). This is private business taking account of the impact of its activity upon the larger community, both on a socio-cultural and environmental level, in which 'stakeholder' links complement 'shareholder' relations and partnerships. Ethical behaviour in this context is expressed by initiatives and investments into activities that contribute to the larger community, for example, the elaboration of infrastructures, the reduction of poverty, or the participation in programmes designed to reduce conflict and injustice.

Recommend reading

HILL (2008): *Part 2*
RUGMAN AND HODGETTS (2002): *Chapters 4 and 5*

2.4

economic integration and trade relations

International trade relations constitute an essential part of relations between states or market groups as parts of a state's potential of power and cooperation policies. These relations are part of International Relations, and are characterized by a multitude of decision-making bodies. Often, this phenomenon of complexity is described as 'polycentric'; some even speak of the 'anarchy of politics' in the political economy. (In contrast, the state is built on a monocentric basis.) Business evolves in this environment, and is regulated by it.

Organizations such as the Organization for Economic Cooperation and Development (OECD) provide the most advanced economies with knowledge and a forum to discuss economic problems and solutions.

World trade is based on a multilateral non-discriminatory trading system, in the past governed primarily by industrialized countries that emphasize World Trade Organization and other multinational trade associations' normalization (setting rules, norms, and standards of conduct on an international level). By the theory (see section 2.2), trade expands by reciprocal tariff reduction and liberalization.

'What is *liberalization* in this context?'

Trade liberalization reduces or abolishes restrictions to trade and investments from outside the country or market grouping, and aims for free trade between trade partners. Since the working of GATT (the General Agreement on Tariffs and Trade, 1947–1995) and WTO (the World Trade Organization, since 1995), essential quantitative barriers to trade, i.e. *tariffs* and *non-tariff barriers* (quotas, licences and technical specifications, among other restrictions), have greatly been reduced or abolished (dismantled). Developing countries liberalize trade regimes to access triad advantages, as the performance of free trade economies has been found to be superior to that of inward-focused economies.

Export-oriented economies such as those of Taiwan and South Korea have experienced formidable economic growth. The same goes for an international firm's performance versus that of locally focused firms. On the negative side, it has been argued that free trade can contain major risks for underdeveloped and developing economies because of a power imbalance with advanced economies' political and corporate authorities.

Trade relations are considered a voluntary exchange of assets. States or groups engage in these relations because of benefits that the trading partners obtain by an optimal allocation of resources (following the theory of comparative advantage explained in section 2.2). At times, resources may not be allocated optimally, for example because of competitive or technological change, or unfair trade practices. On welfare grounds, this may explain and even justify the application of restrictions on trade. These restrictions on trade are used for a reallocation of resources for the mutual benefit of all trading parties (Julius DeAnne, 1990), and for reducing the harm done to certain industries caused by distortions of trade. But the line between welfare and protectionism is fine. It is the aim of the GATT, then since 1995 established as the WTO, to provide a forum for the promotion of non-discriminatory international trade between its participants, mainly via periodic trade rounds and dispute-settlement mechanisms. In this, negotiations are to reduce or abolish restrictions on trade (mainly via the most-favoured-nations clauses that provide states with preferential trading conditions among each other), to homogenize trade documentation procedures, and to provide for legislation on trade. WTO negotiations increasingly deal with services, and have moved to give more power to developing countries.

The protectionist means that are quotas, tariffs, and qualitative restrictions (see section 2.3) serve as main tools in trade disputes, next to propaganda and similar means. The liberalization from such protectionism typically stimulates international business, trade and investment. On the contrary, trade disputes and protectionist measures typically slow down **bilateral relations** (between two states or groups) or **multilateral relations** (between more than two partners), and need to be settled on a bilateral or multilateral level.

One of the favourite teaching cases for trade disputes is one dealing with what was named 'The Banana War'. This is an example of a US case brought to the WTO against the EU discriminatory import policy for bananas from former colonies, i.e. 71 African, Caribbean and Pacific countries. This case is mentioned in all major IB textbooks in one form or another.

The quality of trade relations is measured mainly by the *balance of payment (BoP)*, i.e. a nation's trade deficit or surplus with its trade partners. This BoP is an accounting record of the transactions between a country and the rest of the world over a given period of time. It is comparable to a company's sources-and-uses-of-funds statement. The *current account*, the *capital account*, and the official transactions account are the principal parts of this statement.

- The *current account* gives the monetary value of the international transactions in physical goods, in services, and in unilateral transfers such as gifts or aid.
- The *capital account* shows long-term and short-term transactions like certificates of deposit and foreign exchange. Internally traded goods rank among the largest categories in most nations' balance of payments. Because employment and standards of living appear so closely tied to these inflows and outflows, there is much debate about why particular countries find comparative advantages in certain goods and have different advantages and disadvantages. For example, countries like China and India, first known for inexpensive products, start to compete internationally in high technology products and raise a highly controversial, large amount of trade surplus with their trade partners.

The power of actors (states, market groups, organizations) in the international environment to achieve their objectives depends in general on their geographic position, the natural resources, economic strength and industrial capacity, and the international situation. Other factors may also be the military potential, size of the population, national character and morale, the quality of diplomacy, and the legitimacy of government.

Many of these factors have their importance reduced in the globalized world due to economic interdependence, liberal and democratic values, and the experience of history.

A list of useful variables that influence the quality of trade relations

A. External variables:

- External demands
- Global trends and events
- Policy changes
- Policy initiatives

B. Structural variables:

- Domestic socio-economic system
- Stability
- Political legitimacy
- Working of economies

C. Community variables:

- Attitudes, norms, standards
- Policies of national administrations
- Interest groups and associations
- Formation of supra-national coalitions

D. Institutional variables:

- Formal and informal initiatives
- Negotiations and consultations
- Cooperation structures

E. Policy variables:

- Objectives
- Perceptions
- Evaluations
- Strategies

F. Sociological variables:

- Motivation
- Qualifications of staff
- Cultural and political perceptions

G. Incidental variables:

- Bilateral bargaining

'What is the impact of enhanced trade relations between two or more countries on corporations' performance?'

Trade relations increase the options that firms have to obtain important and possibly less expensive resources and to enter markets that potentially increase revenue and profit. This may be a question of survival in highly competitive sectors, for small innovative companies and for small countries that are dependent on others to see their economy grow. Firms can enhance their competitive advantage through internationalization (We will review internationalization tools and strategies in section 2.6 in detail.) Porter's diamond model (mentioned briefly in section 2.2) names four main conditions that influence a firm's competitive advantage, i.e. factor conditions, demand conditions, related and support industries and firm strategy, structure and rivalry. Also, the model includes two external variables, i.e. chance events such as benefits stemming from innovations and governmental policy such as changes in regulations or policy plans that after factor endowments. This helps in analysing strategies that are employed in 'triad' and other advanced economies. It also illustrates that national responsiveness and local knowledge are key to international performance.

Pitfall

Be careful – while Porter's diamond model applies well to advanced economies' strategies, it is not entirely suitable for the analysis of smaller economies.

'Why and how do corporations then profit from trade relations?'

The quality of trade relations has a significant influence on the *foreign direct investment (FDI)* activities of international corporations. FDI means that firms invest outside their home country, and thus own/control foreign assets. FDI is therefore a much stronger engagement in the international community than international trade that consists of export and import activities only. Over the past three decades, most FDI activity was confined to the triad countries.

The Triad denominates the three major trade and investment partners in the world economy, i.e. the USA, the European Union, and Japan (the definition is currently being enlarged to include Asia, in particular China and India).

Taking it **FURTHER**

> About 80 percent of FDI takes place among triad countries and within their market groupings. Non-triad countries most successfully invest in triad-driven groupings. Economic integration drives FDI activity and performance of corporations that engage in it. Note that FDI is different from portfolio investment, defined as the purchase of financial securities in other organizations for a financial gain when these marketable assets are sold.

In this, trading blocs are the preferential economic arrangement among a group of countries. They may take the shape of:

- free trade areas
- customs unions
- common markets
- economic unions.

The *free trade area* is the least restrictive and loosest form of economic integration among countries. In a free trade area, all barriers to trade among member countries are removed. An example of this is the North American Free Trade Agreement (NAFTA) and ASEAN (Association of Southeast Asian Nations)'s AFTA.

Members of a *customs union* dismantle barriers to trade in goods and services among themselves. A customs union establishes a common trade policy with respect to non-members. For example, a customs union rules trade between Turkey and the European Union. Other examples are MERCOSUR, having moved from free trade area to the customs union, and the efforts of the East African Community (EAC).

A *common market* has no barriers to trade among members and has a common external trade policy. Factors of production are mobile among members. Members of a common market must be prepared to cooperate closely in monetary, fiscal and employment policies. A common market exists, for example, in CARICOM (The Central American Common Market).

The creation of a true *economic union* requires integration of economic policies in addition to the free movement of goods, services and factors of production. Under this union, members would harmonize monetary policies, taxation and government spending and a common currency would be used by all members. The establishment of transnational rules and regulations enhances economic relations and cooperation among countries, economies, business and communities. The European Union is currently the only example of a market grouping striving to attain these goals.

❝The process of monetary union goes hand in hand, must go hand in hand, with political integration and ultimately political union. EMU is, and was meant to be, a stepping stone on the way to a united Europe.❞

(Wim Duisenberg, former President, European Central Bank)
www.europeanfoundation.org/quotes.html

Market grouping results in *trade creation* and *trade diversion* effects, i.e. mainly the impact of integration on import prices, competition, economies of scale (lower production costs from greater production for a vast market), and factor productivity; that is the benefits of regionalism versus nationalism. Diversion takes place when the union is strong enough that non-members decrease exports to members of a market grouping, thus advantages shift from lower-cost external producers to higher internal cost producers.

In an IB exam, you are typically asked to analyse the opportunities that may be explored by the international manager. You remember to explore the issues that strengthen the corporate fit into this enlarged, less uncertain business environment. It calls for the adaptation of:

- *the company's entry mode, i.e. firms may move quickly from exports to investments because of liberalized trade and investment conditions, and differing factor conditions in the members of the market grouping*
- *effects of change which can be an opportunity to access new resources (financial, human, natural), and the simplification of trade policy and tariff structures*
- *strategic planning: uncertainties are reduced in a market grouping in which rules are harmonized, i.e. common rules are set and accepted by the actors in the adhering countries*
- *reorganization which can streamline the firm's cross-border business to raise efficiency within the market grouping (that reduces administration, financial management and other tasks)*
- *public affairs management and lobbying which must be expanded to the decision-making authority of the market grouping.*

The purpose of enhanced trade relations and economic integration is, for international business, to increase sales and profits, enter rapidly growing markets, reduce costs, ensure the benefits of adhesion to economic blocs, and their dynamic flow of trade and investment among them (intra-regional), or its neighbouring countries (inter-regional), to protect domestic and foreign market activity, and to acquire technological and managerial know-how.

> Most international business takes place on an intra-regional level. For example, only 10% of Wal-Mart's stores are located outside of North America.

Taking it *FURTHER*

The European Union constitutes the most advanced form of economic integration. Among its goals are:

- the elimination of customs duties among member states
- the elimination of obstacles to the free flow of import and/or export of goods and services among member states
- the establishment of common customs duties and unified industrial/commercial policies regarding countries outside the community
- free movement of persons and capital within the bloc
- the acceptance of common agricultural policies, transport policies, technical standards, health and safety regulations, and educational degrees
- common measures for consumer protection
- common laws to maintain competition throughout the community and to fight monopolies or illegal cartels
- regional funds to encourage the economic development of certain countries/regions
- greater monetary and fiscal coordination among member states and certain common monetary/fiscal policies.

Recommended reading

HILL **(2008)** *Chapters 1, 6 and 8*
RUGMAN AND HODGETTS **(2006)** *Chapters 3, 15 and 19*

2.5	
globalization and the monetary system	

"An unstable exchange rate means unstable financial markets, and a stable exchange rate means more stable financial markets."

(Robert Mundell, Canadian, Nobel Prize in Economics)

Exchange rates have an ubiquitous impact on financial markets. Financial markets and financial flows have been exposed to globalization from the earliest stages on, and constitute an essential part of international business.

With this, monetary issues are key because they differ from one marketplace to the other. This is why the understanding of currency concepts constitutes the very basis of international management. Also, through the understanding of the foundations of purchase power parity and forward buying, conceptual rules of currency behaviours help get a grasp of how they relate to fluctuations in exchange rates. For your IB course, you are typically required to become familiar with the primary types of currency exposure, and with essential strategies in cash flow management. Another challenge for MNCs is the accounting compliance in different countries and the differences in international taxation across the world.

'Why should I study financial and monetary issues if I want to work in international business?'

International companies face challenges and opportunities that domestic companies can hardly fathom. When a company crosses borders, a new set of rules apply. Currency exposure, cash flow management, varying accounting compliance issues and international taxation laws are all areas the MNE must master. Because currency changes consistently, it is difficult for MNEs to predict their financial future. Yet, it is necessary that they are able to so. Due to this paradox, MNEs must become aware of the impact of their decisions and know their possibilities for dealing with exposures.

Basic Currency Concepts

In order to explore the complex world of international currencies, one must ensure that the foundation for understanding has been securely established. To do this, let us explore some of the basic concepts as interpreted by academic scholars.

The Gold Standard is defined as: 'a standard for international currencies in which currency values were stated in terms of gold' (Czinkota et al., 2005).

Conversely, Eiteman, Stonehill, and Moffett define it as: 'a monetary system in which currencies are defined in terms of their gold content, and payment imbalances between countries are settled in gold' (Eiteman et al., 2007).

Whether the Gold Standard is considered a monetary system or simply a base for which currency values are determined, it is agreed that its relationship to the evolution of human economics has had a profound influence. The Gold Standard served as a benchmark which countries used to determine the value of their currencies in relation to the currencies of other countries. This agreement of a global gold standard was the birth of foreign exchange using a commonly regarded assessment. However, it was abandoned for a more Keynesian approach because the gold standard barely held its promise in regard to a balancing effect.

 Taking it **FURTHER**

The gold standard, originally created as a medium of stability in international monetary transaction, was abandoned by the UK in 1931, by the USA in 1933, and not used anywhere in the world since the 1970s. Governments prefer to back currencies and reserves.

The Bretton Woods system had ruled the system of financial transactions across borders since 1944. It created the obligation for each country to adopt a monetary policy that maintained the exchange rate of its currency within a fixed value – plus or minus one percent – in terms of gold and the ability of an International Monetary Fund (IMF) to balance out punctual distortions of payments.

However, it was found that *Purchase Power Parity (PPP)* has to be taken into account in the globalization of monetary flows: the primary factor in PPP is called the Law of One Price. The Law of One Price is defined as: 'the theory that the relative prices of any single good between countries, expressed in each country's currency, is representative of the proper or appropriate exchange rate value' (Czinkota et al., 2005).

Others define it as: 'an economic rule which states that in an efficient market, a security must have a single price, no matter how that security is created' (InvestorWords, 2006).

Simply phrased, the Law of One Price states that the price of a particular item in one country will equal the same item in any other country. If a basket of goods costs $1 in the USA, and the same basket cost 114¥ in Japan, then the exchange rate between the two countries should be that of $1/114¥ (Eiteman et al., 2007).

Note that unfortunately, the Law of One Price is an economic theory that does not usually prove to be accurate. There are often discrepancies between theory and reality.

All major world currencies are either over-or under-valued in relation to the same basket of goods. This is evidence that the PPP is more theory than an actual representation of truths. As a result of the different currency values and their deviations from the concepts of PPP, international corporations have been forced to develop methods for handling exchange rate fluctuations: ever since the1970s, the world's major currencies have floated in value versus each other, and firms have had to deal with that.

Because currencies fluctuate, companies need to be able to predict future rates. A country that wishes to strengthen its local currency may choose to attract foreign investors by lowering its interest rates. Countries with strong currencies will decide to purchase foreign currencies in countries with low interest rates.

'Does forward rate buying help firms master international financial flows better?'

It helps both parties. However, if there are sudden or unpredicted changes in a currency's value, it can become very damaging for the international companies and investors. Through international financial institutions, companies can protect themselves by purchasing currency in predetermined amounts. Later, if the currency changes unexpectedly, the companies are protected. Buying forward is one form of *hedging* against uncertain currency exposures.

Currency Exposure Types

Foreign currency exposure management is a valuable tool for firms to protect themselves from fluctuations in global currency prices. Exchange exposures include selling products overseas, importing goods or raw materials from abroad, owning foreign assets and making investments in, or receiving investments from, a different currency (Pritamani, Shome, Singal, 2003).

Typical exam question: *What are the primary types of exchange exposure that can be identified? According to Wei (2006), there are four, as follows:*

- *Transaction exposure is the risk that companies face when they have foreign financial obligations. As time passes, exchange rates change. It is common for companies to find themselves with additional debt because of currency changes.*
- *Accounting exposure, commonly called translational exposure, is a risk that applies when a company owns assets in a foreign country. As exchange rates change, so does the value of their assets. When a company consolidates foreign assets into one balance sheet, they may find that the conversion into their local currency will result in the assets being worth less.*
- *Operating or economic exposure is an indirect exposure. This occurs when currency rates change in a way that affects the company through less obvious methods. For example, this can include suppliers who raise their prices because they were affected by another country's currency.*
- *Tax exposure occurs as a result of the required tax payments due in various countries. Although payments to one country are often deductible to another, there are possibilities of double taxation.*

Regardless of the type of exposure, a company must consider all possible methods of protection. To minimize exchange risk, companies can hence use:

- *Risk avoidance*: this means to avoid operating in more then one currency. Obviously, this strategy is impractical because all firms are affected by goods priced in foreign currencies.
- *Risk adaptation*: here a company tries to adjust its business activities by trying to balance foreign currency assets and liabilities and outflows and inflows through forward transactions.

- *Risk transfer:* a company tries to pass the exchange risk to an insurer or a guarantor by an insurance contract. For example, the central bank offers exchange risk guaranties to explorers or importers of some products according to the bank's policies.
- *Diversification:* in order to reduce the impact of exchange rate changes, the company spreads its assets and liabilities through several currencies (Euros, Dollars, etc.).

To generate an efficient strategy against currency risks, management, beforehand and in continuous repetition, has to define the risks which their company faces. This requires appropriate knowledge of foreign exchange risks, accounting practices and economic reality in terms of measuring exposure.

Exposure Management

You will encounter a variety of strategies that an international firm can use to manage its cash flows and protect it from fluctuating currencies.

Two of the most common tools are known as *netting* and *hedging*.

Netting can also be used in conjunction with cash pooling and re-invoicing. These methods are useful to an international firm that is required to consolidate the financial statements from multiple countries. Often in a multinational firm, one location may assist or trade with another of its subsidiaries. Before government reporting can occur, the company that wishes to protect itself from exposure will determine the net balance due to and from each separate operation. By making an accounting adjustment of who owes whom, the corporate office can record the net results.

Note that depending on the number of currencies involved, netting receivables and payables can prevent the company from showing income in countries with undesirable tax implications or those with weak currencies (Risk Institute, 2000, http://riskinstitute.ch/).

Additionally, Kirt Butler's illustration of the concept of netting is very helpful if you have difficulties in understanding this: in his book *Multinational Finance* (Butler, 2004), he shows the relation between international subsidiaries both before and after the netting of their respective cash flows very clearly.

The second strategy is known as *hedging*. The aim of hedging is to secure particular currency rates, thus safeguarding from future changes. Users of hedging methods use the following arguments to support their case (for example, in Marshall et al., 2006):

- Reducing risks in future cash flows improves the planning capability of the firm.
- Reducing risks in future cash flows reduces the probability that the firm's cash flows will fall below a necessary minimum.
- Managers need this strategy for the competitive advantages over the individual shareholders for the foreign currency risks.
- Managers need this strategy to take advantage of and enhance the firm's value through the disequilibrium market condition.

Pitfall

Do not forget that hedging strategies cannot be applied for conditions which do not allow investors to quickly access the effects of exchange rate changes on the firm's value.

The opponents of hedging strategies make the following arguments (for example, detailed in Dewenter et al., 2005, and referred to in the main textbooks):

- Shareholders are much more capable of diversifying the currency risk than the management of the firm.
- The impact on value is a combination of the reduction of cash flow and the reduction in variance.
- The hedging strategy may not be in the best interests of shareholders because the goal of the firm is to maximize the profits.
- Managers could not outguess the future markets: the expected net present value of hedging is zero.

Hedging will increase the cost of protection in operating and interest expenses, even though it appears in the income statement as a highly visible separate line item or as a footnote. The international manager's choice of hedging methodology depends on the individual firm's currency risk tolerance, and its expectation of movements of exchange rates.

Different ways of hedging apply to each of the exposure types. All currency protection devices can be used separately or in combination with one another. The key factors in deciding what strategies to apply will be influenced by the company's accounting and taxation requirements.

Accounting Compliance

Every economically developed country has some form of government reporting requirements. International firms face the complex challenge of complying with the regulation standards for each country where they operate. For example, recent changes in the USA have caused problems for foreign companies operating there or being traded on any of the US stock exchanges. US laws mandate that all such companies fully comply with the Sarbanes-Oxley (SOX) regulations. Unfortunately, when attempting to comply, some companies have found that they are in violation of the requirements of other countries where they operate. Until there is a global standard, MNCs will continue to be caught between the government regulations of their home country and that of the other countries as well as increased expenses.

Taking it **FURTHER**

In an article by Compliance Pipeline News, the cost associated with full SOX compliance is regarded as 'a good investment' (14 December 2004). In contrast, European companies have been seeking exceptions and flexibility in the SOX regulations. Theodore di Stefano of the E-Commerce Times states that the SOX regulations are difficult if not impossible for European companies to comply with, without causing problems for them in their home countries (4 March 2005).

International Taxation

International corporations may be required to pay millions in government taxes. Often a company can find itself in a situation where it is being double-taxed. Several countries can agree to tax jurisdiction and offer deductions to companies that were forced to pay taxes in different countries. However, this is not true for all countries. As a result, the firm may be required to pay taxes in more than one country for the same income. Therefore, every aspect of the planning process must involve a concern for taxes.

Whether the management decision involves import or export, foreign investment, subsidiary operations or franchising, all elements of international business are affected by taxation. Note that there are a great many discrepancies in countries' accounting requirements. For example, the capitalization of finance leases is required in the USA and not allowed in Italy. International managers must be aware of the accounting regulations in every country that the firm operates. Hence, multinational companies continuously analyse new ways to reduce their exposures.

MNCs can be vulnerable in their currency exchanges, cash flow management, cross country taxation and accounting compliance. The complex world of international monetary issues plays a dramatic role in the success or failure of every company that operates in a global economy.

Global cash flow management

One of the key areas of international financial management is global *cash flow management*. Three of the most important ways to do this follow below.

1 **The use of internal fund flows** is when an MNE obtains the monies needed by getting them from internal sources such as working capital, by borrowing from a local bank or from the parent company, as well as by making the parent company increase the equity capital investment.

2 **Funds positioning techniques** are used to move monies from one multinational operation to another. Again, there are three common approaches for this strategy:

- **Transfer pricing**, an internal price set by a company in intrafirm trade to maximize the profits in the low tax rate country and minimize them in the high tax rate country, should be differentiated from the **arm's length price**, which is the price at which two unrelated companies would agree to a transaction under conditions of perfect competition, as contrasted with an intracompany transfer price.
- The **use of tax havens** offers the MNEs no tax or a lower tax rate than in other places, so that they can locate some of their business activities there and thus reduce overall tax payments.
- **Fronting loans** refer to the funds that are deposited by the MNEs for their subs in a foreign country but managed by a third-party international bank, in order to avoid the political risk and currency transfer restrictions from this country.

3 **Multilateral netting** is the payment of net amounts due only between affiliates of a MNE that have multiple transactions among the group, which can be partially netted out among them.

'Are there any rulers of capital markets?'

Regional money and capital markets set rules for MNEs. The *Eurocurrency* is one example: the Eurocurrency market is a set of bank deposits located outside the countries whose currencies are used in the deposits. More than a half of these deposits are denominated in US dollars. Over the years, the Eurocurrency market has been harshly criticized by some economists who claimed that it would contribute to worldwide inflation and also create major new risks in the international banking system.

- The Eurocurrency interest rate: the reference rate of interest in the Eurocurrency market is the LIBOR (London InterBank Offered Rate) which is used in standardized quotations, loan agreements, and financial derivatives valuations. Other examples are the PIBOR (Paris InterBank Offered Rate) and the FIBOR (Frankfurt InterBank Offered Rate).
- Eurobonds and Euroequities: *Eurobonds* are underwritten by an international syndicate of banks and other securities firms, and sold exclusively in countries other than the country whose currency denominates the issue. *Euroequities* are shares of publicly traded stock whose primary exchange is located outside the issuing firm's home country.

On a global level, the International Monetary Fund (IMF) is the key institution in the globalization of monetary flows and its management worldwide. The IMF was founded in Bretton Woods in 1944. Its main missions consist of:

- offering balance of payments support to countries in crisis
- giving financial advice to central banks
- granting loans to less developed countries.

> *When studying IMF tools and mechanisms, do pay special attention to the Special Drawing Right (SDR) which is an international reserve asset 'created by the IMF in 1969 to supplement the existing official reserves of member countries. SDRs are allocated to member countries in proportion to their IMF quotas. The SDR also serves as the unit of account of the IMF and some other international organizations. Its value is based on a basket of key international currencies' (Euro, Dollars, Yen and Pound).*

Recommended reading

CZINKOTA ET AL. **(2005)** *Chapters 7 and 17*
HILL **(2008)** *Part 4*
RUGMAN AND COLLINSON **(2006)** *Chapters 7 and 14*

2.6

internationalization: theory, tools and HR issues

Why and how do firms go abroad?

The Multinational Enterprises (MNEs) are only one form of international business. Typically, a firm opts for a basic progression through the process of internationalization, but it may become extremely performant and powerful in the global business economy.

> In the year 2000, Exxon Mobil's estimated value-added was some 63 billion US dollars, while the estimated value-added for the national economy of Pakistan was some 62 billion US dollars.

The role of management in this progression, to worldwide dominance or simply to profit maximization through foreign sourcing or sales, is crucial in developing international market entry, international expansion, and by extension global strategic planning.

The **Internationalization process** is 'the process by which the economic relations between nations tend to intensify at intervals faster than the economic relations domestically (inside the nation)' (Dictionnaire de L'Economie, 2000, p. 338) and at the same time 'the process by which a company enters a foreign market' (Rugman and Hodgetts, 1995, p. 40).

Internationalization comprises important strategic decisions about the market and location to enter, the mode of entry, the commitment of management to this move abroad and the human resources issues that have to be handled for overseas operations, in developed or less developed countries that may be subject to the flying geese effects (that will be explained below).

Localization decisions need to comprise a focus on:

1 products (adaptation to local needs)

2 profits (reinvestment in a foreign market to create a self-sufficient segment)

3 production (the aim of producing completely in a foreign market)

4 management (local vs culturally trained foreign managers).

The main reasons that make a firm chose one location rather than another are:

- local externalities, education, infrastructures
- research and development (R&D) spill-overs
- opportunity and costs of knowledge transfer
- *transaction costs.*

Therefore, internationalization takes places mainly when the chosen location helps:

- reduce costs
- access rare, new, more efficient or cheaper resources (raw material, human or financial resources, etc.)
- gain market access (possibly even to a market group)
- develop or preserve strategic strengths (through the **first-mover advantage** of entering a market before the competition does; of challenging competitors internationally, through economies of scale, etc.)

and the right location will support competitive advantages vis-à-vis challengers in the firm's market.

You may be asked to distinguish between:

- *a Multinational Company (MNC): a firm that operates in more than one country, with headquarters in one country, and*
- *a Transnational Company (TNC): a firm that coordinates and controls international operations and adapts its structure to localities.*

Through this internationalization, the corporation's value chain is modified: it has to revise the cost/benefit ratio that defines how effective internationalization becomes and which mode of entry will be most suitable. The value chain comprises mainly procurement, orders and invoicing, manufacturing, inventory, service provisions, shipping and all elements of logistics and order fulfilment. The planning, time arrangement and cost efficiency of this chain are crucial for sound international performance.

During the entire process, the firm considers and reconsiders whether and at which stages ownership is necessary and useful, whether the location is adapted to its objectives, and which elements of the value chain can and should remain internalized. Dunning's eclectic paradigm, called **OLI (ownership, location and internalization)**, conceptualizes these considerations. They depend on a large set of information accumulated through the market study, analysing the economic, legal, social, cultural and organizational infrastructure of the firm and the business environment to find the most effective match (including company law, labour and employment law, taxation, knowledge, product life cycles, risk, factor mobility, and more).

The typical process involves step-by-step internationalization along several **modes of entry** through:

- *licensing, franchising, contract*
- indirect export (via agents or distributors)
- export with own representative or sales subsidiary
- local packaging/assembly activities
- *strategic alliance*
- *foreign direct investment* in the shape of, for example, *joint venture*
- *merger* and *acquisition*
- *greenfield*/whole-owned subsidiary investment.

The firm typically enters its internationalization process through the initial *licensing* out of patents, trademarks, or technology to a foreign company in exchange for a fee or royalty. The firm avoids the risks of foreign involvement. In *franchising*, a firm grants the use of a trademark or an asset to a franchisee, which is an independent foreign firm that pays a fee.

> McDonald's, KFC and other food and beverage chains engage in this: the benefit for the franchiser is a rapid expansion, and for the franchisee, the use of a process and a well-established name.

Alternatively, *contracts* allow a firm to offer services (management, technical expertise, operational know-how) abroad for a fee and for a certain period of time; it allows the company to use resources effectively but may represent a short-term mode of entry only. (Similarly interesting are **'turn-key' operations**, in which the firm constructs sites, starts operations, and trains local personnel for a foreign company and then transfers it to that firm.)

The internationalizing firm may also choose exports to seek potential extra sales, for example for surplus production or simply to follow competitors. To do this, it uses a local **agent or distributor** who knows and operates in a particular market. **International trading companies** may be used as agents for some companies and as a merchant wholesaler for others, normally to export as well as import.

Export commission agents represent overseas purchasers, such as import firms and large industrial users: they buy for their foreign customers. *Export merchants* buy goods directly from the producer and then sell, invoice, and ship them in their own names so that foreign customers have no direct dealings with the manufacturer. Alternatively, **cooperative exporters**, i.e. established international manufacturers, sell the products of other companies in other countries along with their own. They both buy and sell for their own account.

The firm can then increase its direct capacity to serve the export market if the **exports** begin to represent a larger share of sales. At this stage, the firm will set up a sales subsidiary or some offices for its sales representative. It will probably also set up a separate export department to manage foreign sales and production for such markets at its headquarters.

Furthermore, over time, the firm will become familiar with the local market; it may begin to move on to foreign production, engaging in local **assembly** and the **packaging** of its product lines. Now, the firm is involved in the host country factor market. *Strategic alliances* involve firms working together on major strategic initiatives, such as in the development of new technology. Strategic alliances also allow arrangements. Here, cooperation is limited to a specific strategic purpose, for example with a supplier to improve quality or logistical aspects.

Joint ventures imply further investment of resources and involvement in the host country. Two or more partners share a project and agree upon what is shared (ownership), how much to share, with whom to share, and how long to share.

However, when two or more full independent companies get together to form a new company, it is defined as a *merger*. An *acquisition* differs from a merger in that 'one party acts aggressively and forcibly takes over the other company' (Cook and Piggott, 1973, p. 192). The merger and acquisition activity in the triad area is very active indeed; the main goal is to streamline operations and investments and to gain advantages vis-à-vis the global competition.

The effects of such consolidation (i.e. combining of assets) can be vast. Stephen Hymer notes that 'multinational corporations, ..., weaken political control because they span many countries and can escape national regulation' (Bhagwati, 1972).

The further the cross-border consolidation goes, the higher is the firm's bargaining power on an international level. For the market regulator, this can be problematic because social problems occur when firms relocate easily, or use their power to achieve dominant market positions that may impede competition and innovation to prosper in free trade conditions. For example, the European Commission (CEC) gave Microsoft a record fine in 2007 for abuse of the dominant the position that, as expressed by a CEC representative, was to make sure that 'Bill Gates does not kill the small rising "Bill Gates" of the future'.

For the firm, internationalization provides local knowledge about the host country environment that, when sufficient, allows for *foreign direct investment* activity such as *greenfield*, i.e wholly-owned, investment.

❝A MNE is commonly defined as a firm headquartered in one country but with operations in one or more other countries, with affiliates of common ownership, resources and strategic vision.❞

(Rugman and Hodgetts, 1995)

Pitfall

When discussing internationalization, do not forget that not all companies use a traditional progressive internationalization process. Born Globals are firms that are international by 'birth' such as global start-ups, instant globalization of high-technology firms, online services, and Information Technology (IT) security solutions. These corporations, often of SME size, rely heavily on their network structure and the diversity of value-added of each component of this structure: the advantages in the use of resources, rocurement, distribution and the cross-border sales characterize this form of diversification and corporate risk-reduction. At the same time, Born Globals need to be run with a global vision and a network relying on the 'know your customer, your supplier and your distributor' principles more than traditionally internationalizing firms.

'Why do firms internationalize, i.e. enter foreign markets?'

- to diversify themselves against the risks and uncertainties of the domestic business cycle
- to tap the growing world market for goods and services
- in response to foreign competition
- to reduce costs
- to overcome barriers to entry into foreign markets
- to take advantage of technological expertise by manufacturing goods directly.

The Role of Management

Once the fundamental decisions of how, when and where to enter markets are made, management dynamism and commitment are crucial to a firm's first steps towards international operations.

" Foreign market penetration requires a vast amount of market development activity sensitivity toward foreign environment, research and innovation. "

(Czinkota et al., 2005)

The firm is seeking **advantages** and benefits that are available internationally. The planning and execution of any internationalization venture must be incorporated into the firm's strategic management process. International trade may be a trigger factor by which new business opportunities are discovered, as analysed in section 2.4. Alternatively, the receipt of information can lead management to believe that international business opportunities exist.

Remember the management differences between proactive and reactive firms. International success for the manager and for the firm is likely to come quicker from proactive behaviour.

The commitment of management is essential in the internationalization process because the process constitutes a long-term engagement. The risks that are associated with currency transfers, politics, government regulations, institutionalization and market competitiveness need to be taken into consideration. Typically, profits will suffer in the short run

Table 6.1   A list of motivations for Internationalization

Reactive	*Proactive*
• Trade barriers are the major reactive motivation: restrictive trade practices can make exports to foreign markets less attractive so the local operations in foreign locations therefore become attractive. • International customers: local operations in foreign locations may be necessary if a company's customer base becomes international and the company wants to continue to serve it. • International competition can cue another major stimulus: if a company's competitors become international and the company wants to remain competitive, foreign operations may be necessary. • Regulations and restrictions imposed by the home government may increase the cost of operating at home; it may be possible to avoid these costs by establishing foreign operations. • Chance occurrence results in a company deciding to enter foreign locations.	• Additional resources: various inputs may be obtained more readily outside the home country. • Lowered costs: factor costs may be lower outside the home country. • Incentives: various incentives may be available from the host government or the home government to encourage foreign investment in specific locations. • New expanded markets: these may be available outside the home country; excess resources can be utilized in foreign locations. • Taxes: differing corporate tax rates and tax systems in different locations provide opportunities for companies to maximize their after-tax worldwide profit. • Economies of scale: national markets may be too small to support efficient production while sales from several combined allow for larger scale production. • Protection of home market through offence in the competitor's home market.

(*Source:* Czinkota et al. 2005)

due to the lack of experience, but start to exceed pre-internationalization profits as soon as transactional and customer knowledge have been gained, and transform into effectiveness, efficiency and competitive strength, aiming for the rise in profitability associated with increasing output value while at the same time decreasing factor costs of inputs.

Human Resources issues

The role of human resources (HR) is to **recruit and retain** an adapted and adaptable workforce for the organization. The more global the company is, the more complex this becomes. Good HR management results in increased effectiveness. It necessitates:

- personnel planning and staffing
- personnel training
- compensation
- the understanding of labour-management relations.

At the beginning of the internationalization process, typically the marketing or sales manager takes on the responsibility and function. Typically, international operations then mean that an export manager is hired, more often from outside rather than through internal promotion.

Then, as the firm becomes more international, HR planning strengthens its focus upon the **needs of the specific markets and functions**. In this,

- local knowledge
- language skills
- adaptability to cultures

are crucial. The HR department will make the choice of sending an expatriate or recruiting a local manager.

In many MNE subsidiaries, locals are employed, with the advantage of fitting into the business environment, and the disadvantage of occasional frictions with headquarter (HQ) strategy. If expatriates are sent out, they need to be chosen for adaptability and self-sufficiency, both culturally and technically, be self-motivated for overseas assignments and have a family happy to relocate.

'How will the expatriate be compensated?'

While the HR department will adapt a manager's base salary to his or her qualifications, responsibilities, and duties, a **cost of living allowance** (COLA) may ensure that the expatriate keeps the same standard of living once abroad. This may involve a foreign service premium, a hardship allowance, a housing allowance and tax equalization. For the transition period, there will be allowances for relocation, mobility, travel, living expenses and language or adapted child education.

Any manager going on an overseas assignment needs to know that social security, retirement and schooling might differ from those in the home country, and that the role of labour unions and that of HR may be different in the host country. This involves, for example, rewards and incentives that may or may not motivate the host country employees, whose educational, cultural and technical background is not necessarily the same. In short, **adaptability** is key when dealing with international HR issues.

The Flying Geese Model

Internationalization targets are not only mature markets. Emerging markets promise considerable gain due to their economic growth, and that of a maturing customer base. MNEs are currently stepping up their presence in the BRIC countries (Brazil, Russia, India and China). The textbooks refer mainly to a model for this issue that has been developed to illustrate how East Asian economies follow the leading model of Japan in its internationalization and that of its corporations: this is called the Flying Geese model. It argues that, within a given industry, trade between countries changes because of enhanced production activity and specialization in the manufacturing of certain goods. This idea of specialization was first introduced by Adam Smith who noted that:

" If a foreign country can supply us with a commodity cheaper than we ourselves can make it, better buy it off them with some part of the product of our own industry, employed in a way in which we have some advantage. "

(cited in Wolf, 2004, p. 77)

The Flying Geese model suggests that areas within Asia catch up with the developed regions and become a part of a hierarchy where manufacturing a commodity will constantly move from advanced countries to less advanced ones. The underdeveloped countries are positioned behind the advanced nations based on their different stages of growth in a wild-geese-flying pattern (Rugman and Collinson, 2006). The main driver in the model is the leader's need to reconstruct its production due to increasing labour costs. There will be a shift in a country's production away from labour-intensive activities to more capital-intensive manufacturing activities. Evermore developed countries transfer their low-productivity production to nations further down in the hierarchy. This pattern is continued between the countries in the lower tiers as well. For example, Japan, as the most advanced East Asian nation moved away from producing textiles, clothing and steel to producing more advanced products such as automobiles and electronics. Other regions of Asia follow the same pattern (South Korea, Taiwan) and the ones that began by producing steel and textiles have already shifted to producing clothing and then to the even more advanced production of microcomputers and high-tech electronics, then entering into research and development (R&D) and innovation. Regions in Asia below them on the hierarchy have taken over and started manufacturing this steel and those textiles.

The Flying Geese model has proven to be a useful tool when describing the regional production patterns in East Asia, for example in Rugman and Collinson (2006). But at the same time, the model has been criticized on various points. One of them is that the emerging economies are not developing their industry competencies in the order of appearance in respect to the model, but they are rather developing competencies across several industries simultaneously.

Recommended reading

CZINKOTA ET AL. **(2005)** *Chapters 11 and 19*
RUGMAN AND HODGETTS **(2006)** *Chapter 12*
RUGMAN AND COLLINSON **(2006)** *p. 584–585*

2.7

international strategy and organizational structures

International business activity and the changing landscape of global markets have a significant impact on the strategic planning of:

- the international firm's business entities
- the ways in which the business organizations should be structured to provide a framework for carrying out an effective and efficient decision-making process
- how to effectively control its operation.

The simple fact of internationalizing and of going global reflects a business orientation based on a belief that the world is becoming more approachable, possibly homogeneous for a particular product or service; this belief has become stronger with the appearance of emerging markets around the triad countries, where hundreds of millions of people share a similar educational background, preference and spending habits.

The company can increase its performance by adapting to the different national markets' needs. When the distinctions are low, products or services are standardized in a variety of countries. On the contrary, when the distinctions are high, products or services of a wide range of sectors are localized.

As a result, companies need to adapt their strategy. This means that management is about formulating strategy across markets to help take advantage of underlying market, cost, and environmental and competitive factors:

- market factors: these factor advantages emerge from large markets with similarities in demand, the cross-border distribution network and technology
- cost efficiency factors: these factors are gained through economies of scale and scope
- environmental factors: these factor advantages may result from the decrease of trade barriers, the harmonization of trade policies and the evolution of technology

- competitive factors: these factor advantages are key to any company, and all firms are looking to set up conditions that favour them. They do so through new market development or new product developments in order to boost growth and market presence, to obtain a first-mover advantage, to pre-empt competitors, or to follow competitors onto other than domestic grounds.

Be careful: this may result in *product standardization* or local adaptation, or a mix of the two.

Most international strategy courses are case study oriented. Their objective is to help you apply some basic tools to analyse the market, the trends on the market and the way in which strategy is adapted to this. The most important basics to study include the PESTEL analysis, Porter's Five Forces, the BCG matrix, the SWOT analysis and some more that are relevant to the particular area of strategy. The case studies then cover the different strategic fields: planning, change, development, and so on. They help you apply the knowledge gained in some other areas.

For example, once having discussed strategic change at SONY, you may be asked to run the same analysis for a different company, i.e. to run one's 'own case study'. This is to help you learn what issues are the most important to look at in any company, what the situation is on the market, what the possibilities are for changing, etc., and – all in all – to recognize general concepts and company specifics in a practical introduction to a future job position as a manager.

Basic Tools

Let us just quickly revise the main tools that one needs for strategic analysis, also known as **strategic audit**, which lay the basis for improvement of business performance to achieve or retain competitive advantage, i.e. advantage that a company enjoys over the competition. Looking at core competencies, analysing the competition, learning from best practice, adding value and defining strategic resources for the long-term, all help identify the right strategy for the right context for a firm. The **value chain** of the company is the start and end point, because it clarifies the primary (essential to creation and delivery) and secondary support activities (increasing effectiveness and efficiencies) of the company.

Here are some of the main tools for the strategic audit:

The **PESTEL** analysis: a framework that distinguishes the examination of the political, economic, social, technological, environmental and legal conditions in a market.

Benchmarking: this exercise helps the firm position itself in the industry and extracts best practice from the business sector or industry that can help improve performance, and explain processes.

Porter's Five Forces: a framework developed by Michael Porter that distinguishes forces stemming from rivalry, the threat of substitutes, buyer power, supplier power, and barriers to entry, for a qualitative evaluation of a company's strategic position in an industry.

The **SWOT** analysis: the examination of Strengths and Weaknesses (both internal factors), and Opportunities and Threats (both external factors), helps the firm understand its position in a business environment, in a strategic audit, that may however be rather subjective. It is hence essential that criteria are well defined and that the weighting criteria are shared with management.

The **BCG matrix**: The Boston Consulting Group (BCG) matrix is the portfolio planning framework that helps classify Strategic Business Units in order to manage them appropriately (for identifying investment and product/service growth strategy). The classification of units is defined by relative market share on a horizontal axis and by market growth rate on a vertical axis. The matrix distinguishes units that can be named 'stars, cash cows, question marks and dogs', facilitating the strategic options for build share, harvest, hold, or divest. The **McKinsey/GE matrix** 'market attractiveness' replaces BCG's 'market growth' (and includes a wider array of factors to take into account!) and 'competitive strength' replaces 'market share'.

The **2 × 2 matrix of country attractiveness**: this matrix, also used on a 3 × 3 scale at times, relates country attractiveness to company strength, and helps establish whether market share, market growth, the presence of competition and other factors can be assessed as favourable in a particular environment, and whether a company can gain enough return compared to the risks that it undergoes by investing, maintaining investments, or divesting in a market: will it dominate the market, harvest returns and grow?

The **Ansoff matrix**: this tool helps define growth potential that distinguishes:

- new or existing products
- new or existing markets

that require

- market penetration *or*
- product development in existing markets *or*
- market development or diversification in new markets,

depending on whether you deal with an existing or a new product.

With a similar objective, the **McKinsey growth pyramid** allows the study of growth strategy through the analysis of operational skills, growth skills, privileged assets, and special relationships that lead to seven growth strategies, from the low-risk option of existing products and existing customers to the high-risk option of exploring new competitive arenas.

❝A strategy delineates a territory in which a company seeks to be unique.❞

(Michael Porter, 1998)

The Strategic Planning Process

In general, a company assesses and adjusts its core strategy through market analysis and internal analysis regularly throughout its internationalization process and beyond. It will formulate a global strategy upon the choice of different competitive strategies (see above) and depending on the target markets. With this information and upon managerial judgment, a global programme can be constructed and implemented.

Assessment and Adjustment to the Core Strategy

Czinkota et al. (2005) opted for a distinction of two levels of analysis:

Market and Competitive Analysis To start with, companies usually investigate the markets and make a thorough competitive analysis. It should be understood that there are often common underlying forces that determine business success, even in different markets.

During analysis, instead of focusing on a single market duly, paying attention to a broad range of markets also provides benefits through risk balance, competitive economies of scale and profitability to gain stronger long-term positions. Through analysing common features like customer requirements and choice factors, forces that drive competition and profitability can be recognized and deeper analysis can then be carried out.

Internal Analysis Major considerations should be put on the company's choice of selecting and allocating the resources as this largely affects it's capacity for establishing and sustaining competitive advantage within the global markets. With the confirmed allocation of resources, rigorous assessments of the organizational commitment would help in expanding the business in the global and regional markets.

Strategic audit and planning is important because they provide a vision to the international company and its organization. A well-communicated strategic vision is motivating and its implementation can be measured and controlled.

In this context, Rugman, 2006 writes about 'goal-setting', visions and other keys to the definition of corporate culture. While all major textbooks contain chapters on international strategy and explain the tools and concepts presented above, their authors do not necessarily present them in the same way and case examples differ. It is therefore beneficial to check out several books for these examples.

In a competitive strategy, the following three factors are often taken into account:

- *Cost leadership*: companies tend to produce identical products through international economies, getting cheaper than their competition through scale.
- Differentiation: companies who focus on this factor perceive there is a uniqueness of one element such as design.
- Focus: companies, like IKEA, usually focus on a single segment to provide customized products, e.g. specific generations or social segments of society.

More and more companies are applying a mix of both cost leadership and differentiation with flexible manufacturing systems. These systems use mostly standard components and total quality management to reduce the occurrence of defects. This can not only customize the products, but also lower their cost at the same time.

In many cases, the above mentioned portfolio models are applied to help choose countries and markets, and can also be used to assess product and business interconnections, segmentation and global programme development. In developing a global programme, management determines:

1 Product offering: companies have to consider whether to produce customized products or not. If so, what kind of customized products should be produced? In many cases, companies tend to produce goods with similar bases while tailoring some other features for different markets to reduce costs.

2 Marketing approach: many companies will implement a marketing approach named 'glocalisation'. It is the approach that sorts out elements that are strategic in nature (e.g. positioning of the company) uniformly around the globe and localizes other necessary tactical elements (e.g. distribution) to better penetrate local markets. One example is Unilever's fabric softener, which uses a common positioning, advertising theme and symbol (a teddy bear) but differs in its brand name (like Snuggle and Cajoline) and bottle size in different markets.

3 Location of value-added activities: companies may want to reduce costs through concentrating activities within a single firm, preventing a duplication of activities in multiples. One example is Texas Instruments' entrance into a strategic alliance with Hitachi to reduce the high R&D costs.

4 Competitive moves: with a regional or global presence, a company may not need to respond to a competitive move only in the market where it is being attacked. Instead, it may compete by draining its competitors' resources in other markets to affect its overall performances.

Organizational Structures

When companies grow and go international, the demands of management require the split of the organization into functions creating values for companies such as production, marketing, sales and R&D. These functions are coordinated and controlled by top management and decision-making tends to be centralized, but that will depend on the international strategy that management adopts. These strategies are well summarized in Hill (2008), and structures are very clearly explained in Czinkota et al. (2005).

Strategies

- Global: create value through cost advantages.
- International: create value through transfer of skills/products to markets that lack those.
- Multidomestic: create value through strong local responsiveness.
- Transnational: create value through transfer of core competencies, local responsiveness and knowledge management.

Structures

The International Division: this is a division in the organization that is at the same level as the domestic one, but is responsible for all non-home country activities.

Global product structure: this structure tends to be adopted by multinational corporations that are reasonably diversified and had originally domestic structures based on product divisions.

Strengths:

- Helps firms overcome coordination problems.
- Provides an organizational context that enhances the consolidation of value creation activities.
- Facilitates the transfer of core competencies.
- Improves cost efficiency through the *centralization* of manufacturing facilities.
- Balances the functional inputs needed for the product and reacts promptly to product-specific problems.
- Is suited to the development of a global strategic focus in response to global competition.

Weaknesses:

- Has a lack of local responsiveness.
- Has an unnecessary duplication of basic tasks such as marketing, sales, production and R&D.

Global area structure: this structure is used for both multinational (multidomestic) and global companies. Area managers take the responsibility for all activities in a particular region and they report directly to the chief executive officer.

Strength:

- Facilitates local responsiveness.

Weakness:

- Duplicates the area, product and functional specialists. Inhibits the realization of location and experience curve economies and the transfer of core competencies between areas.

Global functional structure: some companies are organized by function at the top level. This is the simplest structure where those reporting to the CEO might be the senior executives responsible for each functional area such as marketing, production, finance, and so on.

Strengths:

- Improves the capital productivity of the combined organizations.
- Capitalizes on worldwide knowledge-sharing and achieves economic scales, while at the same time retaining the flexibility to tailor individual products to individual markets.

Global hybrid structure: the structure is organized by more than one dimension at the top level. In this structure, a mixture of the organizational structures is used at the top level.

Global matrix structure: the matrix structure attempts to mesh product, area, and functional expertise while still maintaining clear lines of authority. It is called matrix because an organization based on one or two dimensions is superimposed on an organization based on another dimension.

Weakness: slow decision-making. The dual-hierarchy structure can lead to conflict and perpetual power struggles between the areas and the product divisions, less-than-optimum compromises, delayed responses, and power politics where more attention is paid to the process than to the problem. To avoid the above issues, the company needs to build a flexible matrix structure.

Decision-making organizations

- *Decentralization*: organizations in which decision-making is pushed down to the managers who are the closest to the action, such as a country manager.
- *Centralization*: the top managers make all the decisions at the headquarters and the lower-level managers carry out their directives.
- Coordinated decentralization: the overall strategy is provided by the headquarters and subsidiaries are free to implement it within a certain range.

Pitfall

Often, departments or business units are not subject to the same degree of centralization: for example, finances will often be centralized within the main office and will be flowing from there to the countries and the other way around. Marketing and promotion can be decentralized in that same firm since country managers are closer 'to the action' and are able to make faster and better decisions.

The link between subsidiaries and the headquarters is secured through three main conditions:

- a clear corporate strategy and vision
- effective human resource management
- the integration of individual thinking and activities in the corporate agenda.

The networked global organization will then avoid the 'not-invented-here' syndrome which is the resistance and inefficiency to implement ideas developed elsewhere without having been consulted. This will also avoid problems of effort duplication because of coherence in strategy and structure, enforced by use of:

- the teaching tool: the more experienced people in the company would give instructions and lessons to the less experienced ones
- international teams and councils: by encouraging them to work on new products, for instance
- the intranet/internet: to get faster communications, and avoid a waste of time and time lag with very little or no cost.

Structures in this international organization vary, and can be those of:

- **Strategic leader**: will represent the headquarters' partners. They make an important profit and therefore have more decision-making power.
- **Contributor**: usually, it is a country's subsidiary, which will use its home speciality to produce some part of the final product.
- **Implementor**: in less developed countries, they mainly act in increasing the economies of scale and scope – just for sales purposes.
- **Black hole**: a country where it is difficult for the company to do what it wants most of the time because of government regulations.

For your exam, lecturers like to use MCQs in this field, which may contain questions such as this one:

If a subsidiary benefits from a high degree of autonomy, the system is called:

A. Centralization
B. Decentralization (the correct answer)
C. Coordinated decentralization

Pitfall

In the study of international strategy, organization behaviour, decision-making and control, some concepts are complicated when studied in theory only. Learning them by heart as a theory does not make sense: they are understandable in terms of practical usage when they are applied in a particular situation. Make sure you understand them in the context of case studies and exercises and that you know what to use the concepts and tools for: to focus on what it is but not what it is for is the biggest mistake one can make in this learning.

Recommended reading

HILL **(2008)** *Chapters 12 and 13*
RUGMAN AND COLLINSON **(2005)** *Chapter 8*
CZINKOTA ET AL. **(2005)** *Chapter 12*

2.8	
business operations and international marketing	

International Production and Manufacturing Strategy

Investments in different areas of production and manufacturing depend upon the coordination and location of knowledge centres across borders. They have to ensure maximum production efficiency and improve the firm's competitive advantage.

The main textbooks explain that the ideal formula for this is to strive to reduce costs, add value, improve quality and service, etc.

This defines the strategy that a corporate management will decide upon, in terms of its mode of internationalization (see section 2.6), its mode and location of production, handling and supply.

Manufacturing

When deciding on a strategy for manufacturing, the MNE can either choose to use overseas suppliers and assembly plants, a process that textbooks term *global sourcing*, or it can manufacture locally. In the latter case, the MNE makes use of modular manufacturing or concurrent engineering in order to accelerate the manufacturing process and improve the speed to market. Getting the product onto the market faster can also be done by choosing the right location for the production system, the right layout and an efficient materials handling system such as Just in Time (JIT) (Rugman, 2006, pp. 291–293).

Just in Time inventory: A minimization of stocks/warehousing through the delivery of quality-checked components and goods at the very time needed.

'Where should an international firm produce which part of its good, or all of it?'

In this, you will encounter the dilemma of whether a good should be produced entirely at home, abroad or what component(s) or proportion of components should be produced and assembled in a specific location.

The location decision for production depends on what Hill (section 2.16) categorizes into three types of factor:

- country factors: the factor costs (i.e. labour, capital – cf. section 2.2), political economy, national culture, location externalities, and their impact on costs
- technology factors: the fixed costs of facility set-up, availability and flexibility of technologies to make manufacture efficient, with a minimum efficiency level
- product factors: the 'value-to-weight' ration of merchandise, and adaptability to markets and market segments.

Note that when asked to define the value of a firm's location decisions for production in an exam, remember that there are trade-offs to all decisions. You should analyse them thoroughly. Also, note the learning curve effect of foreign facilities and human resources that can become increasingly efficient with time.

The decision as to where components are to be produced depends on the specialized assets that the firm either needs from outside sources, or owns and does not wish to share (i.e. of which it internalizes the knowledge).

Other determinants are geographic considerations and competencies stemming from national cultures.

Integration

One of the strategies often used by an MNE in order to cut costs, gain control or achieve better effectiveness is to integrate forward, backward or horizontally in the production line (Rugman, 2006, p. 280):

- backward: a producer buying the supplier
- forward: a manufacturer buying a retail company
- horizontal: buying off the competitor.

'What are the advantages of working with independent suppliers instead?'

Instead of integrating, a company may also open its own facilities, or purchase components from independent suppliers. The advantage then lies in the firm's flexibility. Most commonly, MNEs engage in long-term (sometimes exclusive) strategic alliances with suppliers.

Innovative Activities

To stay competitive on an international level, the MNE has to continuously invest in research and development (R&D).

R&D centres help the MNE to collect knowledge through networks with institutions such as governments, universities, regional headquarters, etc. Different types of knowledge are collected, from highly specialized product and market information to data on the manufacturing plants (Rugman, 2006, p. 282), by technical design and development and applied technical development centres.

This knowledge can then be used for the development of products and accessories, and towards the improvement of the process of making the product. However, the main issues for any MNE remain the coordination of the knowledge acquired and the picking of the right location for innovative activities. For example, an MNE might choose to locate an applied R&D centre in the area of their main markets and a technical R&D centre in the same region as their production facilities. This becomes more and more common with the very large MNEs.

'Why does an MNE continue to engage in R&D?'

Newly acquired knowledge helps the MNE to map out its operations and strategies around the world. In this, new product development is key in highly competitive markets, creating new market opportunities and first-mover advantages. The right formula exists when the MNE successfully integrates R&D, marketing and production, and beats its competition. Hill (2008) notes that the following criteria help in this:

- responding to customer needs
- facilitating manufacture
- balancing development expenditure
- a minimal time to market through speed, quality and performance.

International Logistics

Due to the complex nature of international operations, the MNE has to carefully consider all factors that potentially add costs or value to the product from the manufacturing facility to the consumer. It has to look at factors such as:

- time (on the one hand, the coherence with the process flow of every step of production towards assembly, transport and delivery to fit together, and the materials management that needs to take account of distance, time and exchange rates; and on the other hand, the time it takes for transport and administrative procedures associated with it)
- cost
- predictability
- other non-economic factors that could affect the system of transportation (e.g. political considerations)
- the shape, weight and cost of the packaging
- the best location for its storage facilities.

The transportation of goods may take place via sea, air, rail, trucks and/or pipeline.

Note: The most common means of transport for long distances is by container ship. It is also the cheapest means.

The choice of means depends on the above-mentioned criteria and the infrastructure of the region(s) that the goods or component needs to cross on its way to delivery. The design and management of this logistical system that controls the flow of material and goods through the firm's international value chain is crucial. Through proper and cost- and weight-efficient packaging, the firm makes sure that the good arrives safely and undamaged, and that must not be shipped in special, more expensive containers, and does not necessitate extensive loading. In terms of export documentation, the international supply chain manager needs to deal with the draft, or bill of exchange, that is an order from the exporter that instructs the importer or his agent to make the payment at an agreed point in time.

Note that in domestic trade, the buyer can receive the goods without this document. Ordered products will be sent on to an open account and then invoiced.

The *Letter of Credit* guarantees that the issuing bank makes payments upon agreed terms, and the presentation of specific documents.

The *Bill of Lading* is a contract between the exporter and the transporter/carrier indicating the responsibility for the goods accepted by the logistics company that sells the transportation in return for payment. Czinkota et al. (2005) list the types of bills:

- the straight bill of lading is a non-negotiable bill used in prepaid transactions
- the shipper's order bill of lading is negotiable and used for letter of credit transactions.

Both need a commercial invoice, i.e. a bill with basic information concerning the goods and other export documents.

Note that freight forwarders specialize in handling documentation.

International Commercial Terms are uniform for all shipment and sale activity: they are called *Incoterms* (mentioned already briefly in section 2.3, and later again in section 2.9), and are internationally accepted standard definitions for the terms of sale set by the International Chamber of Commerce since 1936 as revised regularly. Here is a list of Incoterms for all means of transport, with a short explanation, that define where each party's responsibility, risk and insurance starts and ends:

1 EXW (ex-works): prices apply only at the point of origin

2 FCA (free carrier): the seller is responsible for loading goods into the means of transportation and the buyer is responsible for all subsequent expenses

3 FAS (free alongside ship): the exporter quotes a price including delivery of goods alongside a vessel at the port and covers the cost of unloading

4 FOB (free on board): the price covers all expenses up to the delivery of goods on an overseas vessel

5 CFR (cost and freight): the price includes the cost of transportation to a named port

6 CIF (cost, insurance and freight): the price includes all these charges to the point of debarkation

7 DDP (delivered duty paid): prices include import duties and inland transportation to the buyer's premises

8 DDU (delivered duty unpaid): only customs duty and taxes are paid by the buyer.

Exam question: In the exam, you may be asked to choose the most appropriate Incoterms for one or more products. Normally, the customer sets the Incoterm, but it can be negotiated. Your choice will depend on the value of the goods, transport means, length and route, standard practice in the countries (for example, in the EU, delivery-type terms are mainly used), regulations in the country of the buyer, negotiation power and/or service interests towards the trading partner, depth of information, trust and past experience, just as does the decision taken by the MNE. But be careful, as the MNE also has to negotiate this with the carrier. Specific group terms (F,C,D) exist that are only used for maritime transport.

'What happens to the goods upon delivery at the port, before final delivery?'

Some storage may be necessary. In the most frequented international ports, public storage facilities are normally available. They differ in size and shape from one location to another.

Note: In Foreign Trade Zones, products are stored and processed and then re-exported without customs duties.

Product/Service Balance

"A product is more than a physical item: it is a bundle of satisfactions (or utilities) that the buyer receives."

(Cateora, 2005)

The MNE has to carefully evaluate the product/service balance. A decision has to be made in terms of how much assistance is needed in order to use the product and how much help will be available to the consumer after the purchase has been made. It is important for the management to clearly define whether a product, a service, or a mix of both is to be sold. This depends on the sector, the competition and the importance of customer satisfaction.

Note: There is a tendency in triad countries, where possible, to look rather for profitability in the selling of the service that goes with a good, than to believe in the money-making capabilities of a good. This stems from the low-cost competition from non-triad countries, for example China and India that, to date, excel more in production than in the services sector.

Marketing Strategy

In order to develop a successful marketing strategy, the MNE has to evaluate the products or services that would thrive in foreign markets; this is called 'international market assessment'. It consists of a process of six phases that analyses several factors:

1. Initial screening: determines the basic needs of the consumers, as well as the potential of the marketplace.

2. Second screening: focuses on the economic and financial conditions. The data is analysed through quantitative techniques.

3. Third screening: looks for the political and legal environment focusing on the entry barriers and government stability.

4. Fourth screening: consists of evaluating the socio-cultural forces such as language, religion, customs, values, working habits.

5. Fifth screening: looks at the level of competition that exists in each market.

6. Final selection: when the companies have got a few targets, they make trade missions to talk to representatives or local officials (Rugman, 2006).

A market assessment demands a great deal of time and energy.

"To reduce the number of analyses to be conducted to a minimum, the international marketer must determine a list of cultural factors specific to its product market(s)[...] Those factors may be specific values, and may relate to verbal and non-verbal communication, education, aesthetics, or the social organization of society "

(Mühlbacher et al., 2006, p. 219)

The market entry decision for the marketer is valid when a favourable risk/return evaluation responds positively to conditions of:

- resources
- cost of adaptation
- organization
- market opportunity
- profitability.

> *The marketer's point of view is slightly different to that of the strategic leadership, of human resources management and other divisions.*

Note: Market entry service providers may be contracted to facilitate the move into a new market/location. For example, a vast number of such providers specialize in market entry into China, and other emerging markets.

After selecting the markets in which the products or services are going to be offered, the MNE has to determine the marketing mix using the '4 Ps' scheme: Product, Place, Pricing, and Promotion.

Product

❝Some products can be manufactured and sold successfully both in the [home country] and abroad by using the same strategies. Other products must be modified or adapted... ❞

(Rugman and Collison, 2006).

The degree of adaptation depends on the type of product that is to be sold:

- Products that require *little* modification are the ones that have to adapt, for instance, only the electric voltage, or the language of the instructions or labels – for example, heavy equipment, laptops, cameras, or cigarettes.
- Other products like automobiles, clothing, cosmetics, pre-packaged food, or even advertising need *a higher* degree of modification in which factors such as economics, culture, local laws, and product life cycle have to be respected.

Pricing

❝[Pricing is] the only element in the marketing mix that is revenue generating.❞

(Czinkota et al., 2005)

The pricing of products and services abroad is highly influenced by government controls that sometimes dictate maximum or minimum prices in order to protect their local markets or their population.

The four main issues in pricing concern are:

- Export pricing: standard worldwide pricing is based on average unit costs of fixed, variable, and export-related costs. Dual pricing differentiates between domestic and export prices. Market-differentiated pricing is based on demand-oriented strategy making it more consistent with the marketing concept.
- Foreign market pricing: determined by corporate objectives, costs, consumer behaviour and market conditions, market structure and environmental constraints.
- Price coordination: standard worldwide pricing may be mostly theoretical. Significant price gaps lead to the emergence of grey (i.e. unauthorized) markets.
- Intracompany pricing: the pricing of sales to members of the corporate family.

Taking it **FURTHER**

Dumping is another pricing technique which is prohibited in most countries, and in international trade. It is an issue of numerous trade disputes. The classical definition of dumping is based on Viner's 'League of Nations Memorandum on Dumping' of 1926. He distinguishes between different kinds of dumping, such as reverse, spurious, exchange, freight and concealed dumping. Efforts are made in order to emphasize that only unfair trade practices are restricted, not trade in general. Viner defines the act of dumping as 'selling at the same prices in different markets', i.e. having a price discrimination between those markets. Dumping in this respect exists in the case of price discrimination between different export prices or in the case of the domestic market being dumped upon itself. In this latter situation, products are sold cheaply on the home market while being highly priced for export. This procedure is called 'reverse dumping'. On the contrary, 'spurious dumping' describes the act of selling products at different prices to different markets. This can evolve from differences that appear in the size of the unit orders coming from different countries, the length of the credits, the extent of the credit risks, or the grades of commodities. Another kind of dumping, 'exchange dumping', is regarded as the export of products which turn out to be very cheap because of a depreciation of the foreign currency. Hereby, a clear price discrimination does not exist. 'Freight dumping' refers to preferential export rates, i.e. transport charges, which normally serve as a natural protection to the domestic industries against outside competition.

Lastly, Viner provides an explanation for a proceeding in international trade called 'concealed dumping'. It implies sales to different markets at the same

(Continued)

prices, despite different conditions and terms of sales. For instance, prices may be kept secret or products undervalued in order to conceal the dumping. Nowadays, dumping is the expression used in economic terms for unfair trade practices based on international price discrimination. It can be described as the circumstance in which the export price of a product is, irrespective of the causes, sold at under-average prices compared to the corresponding product, the 'like product', on foreign markets. This is considered to be an illicit commercial practice because of its incompatibility with international law or with generally accepted rules.

Another important factor is the consumer perception of prices – for example, in some cultures they equate expensive goods with high quality. The currency fluctuations and the price escalation forces, which refer to 'the added costs incurred as a result of exporting products from one country to another' (Cateora, 2005), are issues that the MNE has to deal with (Rugman, 2006, p. 324).

Place

The placement of the product refers to the way in which the distribution is managed. The distribution is the whole process that takes place from the product being finished to it reaching its final consumer. This step may sometimes be hard to standardize due to the different conditions that exist in each country (infrastructure and communications), as well as the consumer-spending habits.

Czinkota et al., 2005 provide a useful list of 11Cs for distribution channel design that can easily be learned by heart and applied to case study examples in exams:

- *Customers*
- *Culture*
- *Competition*
- *Company*
- *Character*
- *Capital*
- *Cost*
- *Coverage*
- *Control*
- *Continuity*
- *Communication.*

An MNE examines several conditions when evaluating a distributor; Rugman, 2006 notes in particular the following elements:

- financial strength (to make sure that they will be operating in the long run)
- how well connected they are (with the consumers or retailers, as well as with the government)
- the number and types of product lines they carry.

The company may then engage in an exclusive distribution system, or allow a limited number or a large number of distributors to sell their product.

'What determines this choice?'

Basic products, such as most food products, need no exclusivity contract. More distinctive, specialized, high-value and luxurious products and brands prefer exclusivity that is in line with the positioning and the product/service combination (see above).

Promotion

The promotion is used to stimulate the demand of a product or a service. Promotional tools are those of advertising or personal selling; and the adaptation required depends on the nature of the product, the local culture and language, as well as government policies (Rugman, 2006, p. 320).

"Advertising and promotion decisions, in turn, must be integrated with the other marketing mix decisions to accomplish this goal."

(Belch and Belch, 1998, p. 61).

Belch and Belch refer to the product or brand image as the goal. All 4Ps should be planned in the same way to run a successful marketing strategy.

The marketer has the option of choosing one of the following two alternatives:

- Concentration: marketing the product or service on a limited number of markets.
- Diversification: marketing the product on a large number of markets, and often early in the internationalization phase of the firm and its product life cycles.

The case of services

A service is a deed, a performance, an effort. Services and goods can complement each others'. Nonetheless, some services are so-called 'standalone' services (i.e. able to cover/serve a full comprehensive system):

- Tangible: food, drinks, cars, books.
- Intangible: communication, reservation, car rentals.

Global transformations in the service sector are frequent due to many changes in the environment: for example, a reduction in government regulation or technological advances that cause a modification in the cost of communication, and other modifications of the marketplace through globalization. This creates several challenges and opportunities for international corporations, and once more, adaptability and responsiveness to the ever-changing international business environment is key. Some challenges that you may need to explore concern data collection, privacy and piracy issues (for example, in the software and e-commerce sectors), the global regulation of services that is a core issue at the World Trade Organization (see also section 2.11), other e-commerce issues, in particular easy, interoperability, the digital divide between those who have access and those who don't, and wide-reaching communication impacts such as reputational risks through the internet. Engineering, insurance, communication, teaching, consulting and tourism are international services that can be sold over the internet and by traditional means. Some text books note that internet-sold services target people's minds (e.g. arts, religion, consulting) and bodies (e.g. healthcare, fitness, restaurants), while traditionally sold services target physical possessions (e.g. laundry, landscaping) and intangible assets (e.g. banking, research): this distinction has changed already and will continuously need attention.

Recommended reading

CZINKOTA ET AL. (2005), *Chapter 14*
HILL (2008), *Part 6*
RUGMAN AND COLLINSON (2006), *Chapter 10*

2.9

risk and uncertainities

Risk is seen as danger and opportunity combined. The complexity of international business is a business risk in itself that must be outweighed by business opportunity. Only when the evaluation of risk and return show a more significant weight for the latter than for the former will a company make investments and run operations internationally.

International business courses increasingly make reference to global risks and their management, and include non-traditional risks in the assessment and analysis of opportunities for international operations.

'What is the difference between risk and uncertainty?'

A risk is typically defined as a function of the probability of an event happening that would cause disruptions or harm business activity and operations, and the impact of such an event. The risk is hence considered as probabilistic, i.e. this type of event has happened before, can be compared with this history, and a probability can be calculated. It is then part of the manager's subjective judgement whether this risk is dealt with, and how. An uncertainty, in contrast, cannot be calculated, because it is not amenable to prediction.

"Operational risk management is situated at the core of both event and business risk."

(Suder, 2006)

Before 9/11, terrorism was part of political risk assessment, but restricted to national or foreign market analysis. Global terrorism has created uncertainty, and has forced companies to revise their scope and tools for risk management. Indeed, roles have evolved due to this development, and Chief Financial Officers (CFOs) see themselves increasingly taking the responsibility for this type of risk. A variety of risks must be assessed and managed by the firm, so that *vulnerabilities* can be reduced. This has to be a continuous and adaptable process.

'What types of risk do companies deal with?'

You are most likely going to study the following topics (one or both):

1 **Internal** risks of the company – for example, cultural, digital.

2 **External** risks of the company – for example, economic, political, terrorism, country risk.

The way companies are facing and reacting to the risk depends on the company culture, the home and/or host country culture and/or the management style, often coupled with the owner's philosophy.

Hofstede's analysis of cultures (see section 2.3) extracted a dimension that he termed *uncertainty avoidance* and that is useful for the study of these behaviours: the extent to which people fear uncertainty and attempt to avoid it.

While much debate surrounds the general validity of his analysis, it provides you with important concepts that are appreciated in the classroom discussion.

> Hofstede demonstrated that the Uncertainty Avoidance Index (UAI) allows us to compare cultures of the highest UAI, such as Greece, with those of, for instance, Singapore with a low UAI.

In *digital risk*, also defined as high-tech risk, the risk originates in information systems' inherent tendency to depend on digital and cyber technology. Main concerns focus on information theft or reluctant transfer, information disability, system destruction or infection, and spread more or faster through regular use of e-mail, internet, Wi-Fi, Bluetooth and USB keys. Causes for crisis are therefore mainly systems malfunctioning, the failure of adding new software to the system, or human error.

> Breaches of computer security registered in companies result in the loss or theft of employee and customer information (identity theft). In the UK, the cost of information security in overall industry is estimated at around 10 billion pounds a year, and has increased by around 50 percent since 2004.

The increase in the risk of unexpected attacks causes high costs of prevention. It may necessitate R&D to elaborate technologies that would prevent the use of unauthorized devices, dedicated links, virtual private networks, encryption, education and corporate awareness, punishment and constant vigilance.

In political risk, three categories will be of main interest to you: they are ownership risk, operating risk, and transfer risk. They stem from conflict and violent changes, such as:

- coups d'état
- expropriation
- confiscation
- domestication
- local content regulations
- Intellectual Property Rights.

Indeed, scholars have now started to look into the role that international companies play in this field.

Country risk analysis examines the probability of non-market events (political, social and economic) resulting in financial, strategic or personnel losses to a firm that engaged in foreign direct investments (FDI) in a specific country and its market.

A generic **political, economic, social** (or 'socio-cultural') and **technology (PEST) framework** is used to:

- map out particular competitive environments or investment contexts for firms at the regional or national level
- compare country conditions
- build future scenarios in order to understand short-term and long-term threats and opportunities.

Political risk, as defined above, is a main part of what is termed as 'country risk', although globalization has necessitated this risk to be assessed on a global level in addition to this country level. Typically, this risk is separated into two categories:

- *Macro political risk:* a risk that affects all foreign enterprises in the same way.
- *Micro political risk:* a risk that affects selected sectors of the economy or specific foreign businesses.

Economic rules and regulations potentially put the survival of a company at risk. Regulatory risks include changes in tax policies.

Here are some examples of very specific security risks:

- Economic/white-collar crime: this is an illegal act committed in the context of lawful occupation. It generally involves deceit, deception, manipulation and a breach of trust. It does not rely on physical forces. Its primary goal is the acquisition of money, property or power.

- Espionage: this is the intrusion of one company or organization in another company's private 'vaults'. It may consist of copying or stealing formulae or products. Efficient measures against espionage are the Economic Espionage Act (1996), and coherent legislation.
- Piracy: this deals with the copying of copyrighted materials by unauthorized means.

The three main forms of piracy are:

- ○ *Counterfeiting*: the unauthorized recording of pre-recorded sounds, or duplication of original artwork, labels, trademarks and packaging.
- ○ *Pirating*: the unauthorized duplication of sounds or images only from a legitimate recording.
- ○ *Bootlegging*: the unauthorized recording of a musical broadcast on radio, television, or a live concert.

The main solutions are again found in legislation and law enforcement, which includes, for example, copyright treaties and the World Intellectual Property Organization (WIPO).

- Burglary: taking money or merchandise without violence is called burglary. Measures to counteract burglary focus on:

- ○ target hardening: paying attention, and using locks, alarms and surveillance devices
- ○ reducing the value of the merchandise.

- Robbery: the threat or act of an attack against people with weapons to take money or merchandise defines robbery. Situations may consist of cash handling, cash transportation, opening or closing routines or cash-room protection. Other measures consist of:

- ○ making stores less attractive
- ○ robbery prevention programmes.

- Labour disputes: these happen within the labour–management relationship. Measures may consist of:

- ○ negotiation with the Trade Union
- ○ a checklist: including moving property most likely to be damaged well back from the perimeter, securing all doors and gates and securing non-strike people
- ○ a pre-strike plan, including the education of all management personnel.

- Terrorism: this has long been part of political risk analysis, but has obtained increasing attention through the phenomenon of global terrorism as defined by 9/11 in 2001. It causes:

o an interruption of business activities
o a loss in revenue, markets, customers and partners
o a hindrance to factor mobility
o an increase in the cost of travel insurance (air travel) and other risk insurances.

The global supply chain under conditions of uncertainty

Supply chain management is one of the main and most visible areas of international business in which risk and uncertainty are studied. Economic impacts, corporate responses and strategic lessons become apparent in this area.

Exam tip

In the exam, you may be asked to analyse a supply chain management case study that may require identifying the locus and modalities of risks, and the risk management responses for that firm.

Friedman's 'Dell Theory of Conflict Prevention'

Friedman has forwarded the much-cited theory, upon research with Dell, that two countries that are both part of a major supply chain (like Dell), will never fight war against each other while having interests in that supply chain. The high risk premium is of main significance here. Global terrorism attempts to break this chain, so as to disturb the established global order and its:

* instantaneous exchange of information
* accelerating movement of currency and investment flows
* interdependent physical movement of goods, raw materials and intangibles with high increases of nodes of interconnectivity due to advances in technologies.

'Why is the supply chain so vulnerable to risks?'

The supply chain is vulnerable because highly developed economies, shifting towards service- and knowledge-driven economies, are more and more dependent on supplies from other countries and their primary (agricultural) and secondary (production, industry) sectors to maintain financial and commercial flows within and throughout the triad, and beyond. The supply chain is:

- the most vulnerable area for any business involved in trade
- subject to physical and virtual disruption (computer technology)
- much more vulnerable than fixed corporate assets
- causing transportation and logistics to face the highest risk levels.

In contrast to traditional risks, global, non-traditional risks (such as global terrorism, pandemics, etc.) require collective responses from all stakeholders in and around the company.

Globalization and supply chain management

- Globalization created vulnerabilities to supply chains, border security and brand management.
- Some companies shortened their supply chains to reduce uncertainty.
- The more internationally diversified the supply chain, the greater the level of risk.

Supply chain re-evaluation and tools for vulnerability assessment

These:

- form a cross-functional global supply chain development team
- identify needs and opportunities for supply chain globalization
- analyse the 'fit' of your current supply chain with your operational requirements
- determine commodity/service priorities for globalization consideration based on needs and opportunities
- identify potential markets and suppliers and compare to current ones
- evaluate markets and suppliers, and identify the supplier pool
- determine the selection process for suppliers
- formalize agreements with suppliers
- implement agreements
- monitor, evaluate, review and revise as needed.

The main effects and tendencies in supply chain management illustrate the challenges in terms of risk and uncertainty management.

Shortening supply chains

- This gives more control, visibility and quicker corrective action.
- Longer, more complex supply chains add uncertainty that must be mitigated through management action.

The shortening of supply chains may lead to the loss of efficiency and value.

The Repatriation of the Supply Chain to 'Safe-Haven' Countries

- There are different levels of risk due to geopolitics and government or industry initiatives.
- Shorter or regional supply chains are mostly more vulnerable to the regional forces of recession.

Inventory Buffer

- Size depends on the length and location of the supply chain.
- Increased inventory requirements add to more costs in securing the supply chain.
- Repatriation allows for a smaller, less expensive inventory buffer.

Side effects increase the terroristic threat

- There is a loss of customers due to miscalculations in lead time.
- There is an increase in regional trade and reduced global trade due to national security protectionism.

Supply Chain Outsourcing

- There is an advantage in division of labour, specialization and discharging the manufacturer and/or distributor.
- There are gains in supply chain productivity.
- There is an enhanced level of security provided by the manufacturer (McIntyre and Travis, 2006).

The true challenge in supply chain management is that of Supply Chain Visibility. Visibility is necessary to establish control, because it allows for the deletion and resolve of irregularities and inefficiencies. One solution can be offered by the use of RFID (Radio Frequency Identification Technology) that can significantly increase visibility for the company and customs, but few other external actors. Another solution is the flexibility of supplier contracts and partners that enhances resilience, i.e. ensures that operations and supplies keep going even in times of crisis or disaster.

Be careful: while it is easy to prove that technology improves efficiencies in the supply chain management, do not forget that all supply chains managed by computers are at risk at every level of the chain. Inadequate backup of data is the most salient risk as they cannot be retrieved. When the system is down, the entire chain is in disarray. This is an extremely attractive target for cyber-terrorism.

In the area of logistics and transport, risks are most prevalent. For example, for the maritime mode, risk managers assess that with this means of transport:

- it is historically vulnerable, but the least costly
- it has little security available on the high seas and has a relatively predictable route
- ships hold a large amount of all kinds of goods
- there are risks of environmental disaster
- piracy still presents a problem for commerce (for example, around Malacca and Indonesia).

A railroad system will imply that trains are easily disrupted, that there is little security on predictable routes, and extensive damage can be caused to the global economy in terms of lost productivity and confidence levels. Also, terrorists could attack the population and the economy at once (for example, the Madrid terrorist attacks in 2005). In addition, trains often also contain hazardous substances, increasing the risk level.

It can be argued that an intermodal transportation, i.e. the use of more than one mode of transport, would be most sensible. However, risks are elevated whenever there is a transfer of ownership or responsibility. Another disadvantage is that this mode is difficult to regulate. Nevertheless, this is often the only option for global trade. Within this, the company is careful to choose the right Incoterm (see section 2.8), and to minimize the cost of security in coherence with the risks assessed. These costs have a direct effect on shareholder value, regard higher levels of inventories, and influence the costs of technology and the costs of regulation necessary for security.

Risks in the field of negotiation

❝Information is a negotiator's greatest weapon.❞

(Victor Kiam (1926–2001), US businessman and
former CEO of Remington)

In negotiations, two or more parties are implicated and the way those parties negotiate may differ. This is a major risk for the progression of internationalization efforts of a corporation, or its partnering capabilities.

In negotiations, the main influencing factors that one needs to be familiar with are:

1 the amount of authority that the negotiator has to approve agreement

2 the objective of the negotiators

3 language

4 the use of written documents

5 perspective on time.

Negotiation between two MNEs

- Both MNE managers have to evaluate their position and the one of the other group.
- Managers have to understand the 'modus operandi' of the other firm and then choose their negotiating style.

Negotiation between an MNE and a government

It is important that the MNE:

- understands the political, economical and social policy objectives
- identifies levers of power
- identifies the structure, network and agencies through which the government operates
- understands its negotiation style and tactics, and the motives driving the actors.

The bargaining strengths of an MNE are in such cases the ownership advantages stemming from technology, products, services, infrastructural contributions, managerial expertise and capital.

In the case of negotiation between two MNEs, look at General Motors and Toyota's 1980s joint venture negotiations, or any more recent one. In the second case of negotiation between an MNE and a government, an example is General Motors negotiating with United Automobile Workers and Mexico in 2007 concerning layoffs at its brake production sites. The bargaining strengths of a government stem from the consumer market, economic and political stability, sources of capital, tax breaks, and (sometimes specific or low cost) labour force. One example is corporations' negotiation of surface rights for oil, gas or other mineral wells in Alberta, Canada, in compliance with the Alberta government's rules and regulations.

Negotiating with partners

Negotiation often includes a third kind of partner (stockholders or interest groups). As an example, during the Apartheid era, many MNEs stopped doing business with South Africa because of the pressure of investor groups. In certain business environments, interest groups and individuals can have a significant amount of power. Also, being a member of WTO, NAFTA or other big trading groups can interfere in negotiations and shape relations between negotiating parties.

"Let us never negotiate out of fear. But, let us never fear to negotiate."

(John Fitzgerald Kennedy (1917–1963), 35th US President)

Reducing risks of failure in negotiation means knowing the 'acceptance zone', an area within which a party is willing to negotiate. When the acceptance zones of the two parties overlap, there is common ground for negotiating. If not, then there will be no end. They have to listen to each other and discuss, and to make some changes to their respective bids and offers to adjust the acceptance zones, and finally reach an agreement. For example, it is not possible to state what the final price will be because this will depend on how willing each side is to concede ground to the other.

Corruption, transparency and other cultural causes of uncertainty

Some business cases deal with the sensitive issues of corruption that international business comes across, i.e. the abuse of public power for private benefit. Corruption spans from the small scale to the very large scale, for a few dollars or advantages to billions of dollars. In India, a few extra dollars may get you onto a train that is overbooked. A president of Indonesia was accused of corruption, receiving more than 15 billion dollars. Both examples illustrate corruption. The extent of corruption is measured by the frequency and value of corrupt payments and the resulting obstacle imposed on business. A survey in 2004 shows that the least corrupt countries are Finland, New Zealand and Denmark; and named Bangladesh and Haiti as the most corrupt countries at that time. Another survey shows a clear correlation between corruption and income, in that poor countries tend to have the highest incidences of corruption.

In this context, transparency is clearly an issue for companies. Clear consistent policies and the application of legislation applied in the governance of business management and partnerships allow for a sound public image. In low-income, developing and emerging markets, transparency is also more of a problem, and is difficult to install because of a lack of legislation and control.

Systems and cultural specific such as *Guanxi* also make negotiation complex and increase the risks of failure and the uncertainty about outcomes.

Taking it **FURTHER**

Guanxi means 'informal, reciprocal obligation networks'. This Chinese term is a very good example of globalization, which is local as well as global. It is a very important and popular phenomenon in China (local). Yet, it is known by more and more foreign business companies and people that adapt to and also adopt this networking theory (global). Although there are similar phenomena in foreign countries, Guanxi is a key success factor for doing business in China. Chinese business people will voluntarily assure you that ... 'without Guanxi, you cannot get your business done ... or you have to pay additional amounts of money.'

Risk Management

International business can use strategic integrative techniques, protective and defensive techniques, or a combination of both, to manage its risks of going or being abroad. Integrative techniques are strategies designed to help a multinational become part of the host country's infrastructure. The objective is to help the company blend into the environment and to become less noticeable as a 'foreign' company. To do so, an MNE can use a name that is not identified with an overseas company, develop good relations with the host government, produce locally or contribute to the community in the location.

Protective and defensive techniques are strategies designed to discourage a host country from interfering in multinational operations. Basically, the aim is to fight against protective and defensive measures which aim at fostering 'non-integration' into the local environment. An MNE has many ways to keep the government from interfering, or to reduce the impact of that kind of interference. It can delocalize its R&D, so that if the government takes over the company, the R&D will still be safe. It can limit the role of local employees to non-vital operations, so that if the government seizes the company, it will not be able to operate it. (However, it will lose out on local knowledge in that case). It can also raise as much capital from the host country and local banks, so that if the government decides to nationalize the corporation, it will have important debts to pay. It can diversify the production in several countries so that the production will be 'resilient' even if one operational location becomes 'redundant'. These strategies are often combined integration and protective/defensive techniques.

Disaster management

Disaster management constitutes a type of occurrence which may be system-induced in the sense that it is an inevitable outcome, at some time or other, of the way that a complex system with multiple interactions operates. The only certainty is that disasters *will* occur; but the timing and perhaps the periodicity is obscure.

These disasters tend to occur in complex, interconnected and interpenetrated systems which are highly reliable under conditions of normal operation, but in practice are vulnerable and may succumb to certain types of attack because of the very tightness of their internal bonding. In this case, wrong-doing is not as a result of random, unpredictable and exogenous shocks, attacks and incursions, but it is a consequence of a complex string of events, antecedent conditions, and small but cumulative defects and deficiencies in operating systems (Weir, in Suder, 2004).

The risk of disasters happening is quantifiable and determined through historical precedent (see above). It is measured as a probability and included in the determinations not only of insurance, but is also used to weight the calculated return on investment. The main types of international business risk are political, competitive, monetary, foreign exchange-related and transactional.

Businesses determine their courses of action based upon risk assessment. With equal levels of risk, a company will choose the course of action with the greater return.

The nature of disaster is prone to uncertainty, i.e. it is a consequence of the lack of historical knowledge on the manifestations of a certain threat and its multiple consequences. Uncertainty is always present in the global environment, and can disrupt sound risk management modes because of unexpected functions or events. Businesses prefer certainty to risk and risk to uncertainty. The risk condition is dependent on managerial decisions.

Recommended reading

RUGMAN ET AL. (2006), *Chapters 4 and 13*
HILL (2008), *Chapters 2, 3 and 19*
CERTO AND CERTO (2006), *Chapter 7*

2.10

knowledge management in international business

The issues of knowledge management are increasingly taught in international business courses, simply because knowledge management is more complex and complicated when the organizational structure of a company is dispersed. It has also gained importance since the mid-1990s, because firms recognize that value is preserved and added when knowledge is held and transferred throughout the company and its stakeholders. The newer editions of textbooks therefore include chapters or sub-chapters in regard to these issues. Rugman et al., 2006, write for example that large MNEs with good knowledge management networks excel in scale and scope advantages and innovativeness.

In this Knowledge Management (KM), an enterprise consciously and comprehensively gathers, organizes, shares and analyses its knowledge, i.e. its resources, documents, and people skills. Knowledge Management in itself is an evolution of information management and information technology, and follows the strong school of belief in total quality management: these concepts have increasingly converged in the past few years. KM is directly related to corporate/strategic intelligence using specialized groupware, networking and business intelligence products that help firms develop, retain and transfer knowledge.

'What is 'knowledge' in management and business terms?'

We distinguish 'data' (facts, figures, statistics) that can be processed to become 'information'. Knowledge then implies that this information is applied to ideas, innovations, skills and assets that are acquired by study, investigation, observation, or experience. This knowledge is utilized to create opportunity and to reduce the resources typically engaged to come to the best decision in a given business or operational context.

The 'people' factor is hence just as important as the data factor is. This is the reason why you will find that a distinction of knowledge into two categories is useful. They are interlinked, and comprise:

- *tacit knowledge*, stemming from people's intellect, intuition, education and experience, and that is rather informal
- *explicit knowledge* that is codified and interacting information in databases, documents etc., and that is formal.

A knowledge programme will process both categories so that knowledge can be developed and transferred. The objective is to use this knowledge as an asset, as social capital, social networking and a tool for motivation and influence across stakeholders. This means that knowledge has to be shared efficiently and that it is possible to adapt management to it, for better learning from one another.

What are the main motivations for firms to adopt KM tools?

- *reduce cost*
- *reduce risks*
- *reduce time*
- *enhance speed of innovation*
- *enhance efficiency.*

KM tool kit and audit management

❝'Management' is getting things done through other people.❞

(Peter Drucker, father of American Management)

Key success factors in KM are the right methods and tools for knowledge – development and learning. In course work and in your exam preparation, students of all levels need to focus on these. This means that one studies the manner in which the international company collects, leverages and uses knowledge most efficiently in the different parts and entities of its business and its locations. Only when this is managed well can a company aspire to using this intellectual asset for its *competitive advantage*.

❝At Lafarge we try to apply 'project/action' perspective to integration. We use systems and procedures, as well as networks, as the means to integrate – but we make sure that the actual integration process is adapted to each unique case [...].❞

(José-Maria Aulotte, Director of Integration, Lafarge Group, www.lafarge.com, 2007)

Methods and tools have to be adapted inside a company, and be used in, for example, a merger so as to make people share their knowledge with others, or in intercorporate alliances, partnerships and ventures. Here is a list of the most essential tools that you will need to know, with a short explanation:

- **After Action Review** (AAR): a discussion of a project or an activity, enabling the involved persons to learn from themselves what happened, why it happened, what went well, what went wrong, what needs improvement and what lessons can be learned from the experience.
- **Collegial coaching**: professionals share their expertise and provide one another with feedback, support and assistance; this helps refine present skills, learn new skills and solve tasks. There are five functions of collegial coaching: Companionship, Feedback, Analysis, Adaptation and Support (developed by Showers in 1984).
- **Yellow Pages**: an early tool in KM history. Also known as expertise locators, (mostly online) staff/corporate directories include details about knowledge, skills, experiences and interests. This semantic system allows for search and retrieval, with many benefits for communities of practice. For example, McKinsey & Company uses its own corporate Yellow Pages.

- **Good or best practice**: common practices such as instruction manuals or 'how-to' guidelines then help identify good and best practices, to learn from others and reuse/adapt knowledge to one's situation, not reinventing already existing methods or tools, but rather benefiting from accumulated experience. The best way to share knowledge is 'on the job'.

> **"When their management asked us what we were proposing, we replied 'We've no intention of controlling your way of doing things. On the contrary, we want to learn from your experience and your practices'."**
>
> (Michel Bon, Chairman and CEO, France Telecommunications, on France Telecommunications' approach to Orange CNNmoney, 2000)

- **Training**: in-company or external training courses use the existing expertise as instruction material, to share experience and discuss knowledge with others.

More tools exist that you will be able to review, in more detail, below, in particular that of the *Balanced Scorecard*. Before that, remember that most of the tools and methods used by organizations are supported by software for efficiency. This is essential for MNEs that deal with knowledge in a great variety of structures and locations.

> At BMW, about 5000 workers are engaged in Research and Innovation Centres that are organized in project teams for car and motorbike development. World- and team-wide domain-specific knowledge can be accessed through its IT and web-based Knowledge Centre with information collection, organization, secure distribution and collaborative features, using Yellow Pages, semantic networks, search engines, eyes (monitoring), agents and knowledge trees for overviews.

'What are the emerging trends and technologies for KM?'

KM can be a great asset when well managed. Business intelligence makes knowledge management a skill when it allows the sharing of the most relevant and highly targeted information (not the biggest quantities but the best quality!), filtered for the interests and needs of particular users. This means that technology at the service of KM must permit the targeting and filtering of relevant information only, to save time and resources because one needs not read potential insignificant information. In this, a processor and/or a controller need to act. This may be a person, or an automated process, depending on the organization (size, type of information).

Technologies set the trends for efficient KM. Starting with the above-mentioned Yellow Pages or the IBM Lotus Notes, KM technology has become more and more sophisticated recently. For tacit knowledge development and transfer, tools include unrestricted online bulletin boards, chats and expertise location. Socialization tools help transfer tacit to tacit knowledge, and to capture it at the same time (e.g. in team meetings). The more articulate this tacit knowledge is, the better it can be externalized to explicit knowledge (e.g. through elicitation). For explicit KM, search and classification remain top priorities. The more a person puts his/her expertise down in writing (e.g. in email or reports), and the more this is filed, the better the knowledge can be shared and transferred, once it has proceeded through this classification mechanism. Ideally, when one then reads the (filtered, relevant, adaptable) explicit knowledge, it becomes possible to integrate and internalize it, i.e. to add the knowledge of others to one's tacit knowledge and come to good practices with it, yet again shared with the community. Technology proposes specialized brainstorming tools, groupware, wikis and other applications that help this transfer mechanism, and enhance the perception that a mental model, values or other important factors are shared. This is essential because people need to be happy and ready to give and absorb knowledge. Technology provides portals, meta-data, filters, citation clauses, peer-to-peer mechanisms and taxonomies (the hierarchical organization of information) to ensure quality and support knowledge mapping efforts adapted to the business process.

> **Pitfall**
>
> *Make sure that you understand the difference between explicit and tacit knowledge, and the manner in which management can use both. This is not always easy. The human factor is very important in KM!*

The success of Knowledge Management is strongly dependent on management variables such as management style, corporate structure, the leadership skills of top management and the firm's organizational structure: it is important that everyone in a company knows what structure and community he/she belongs to, if it is centralized or not, if innovative thinking is encouraged, as these will determine motivations and behaviours. It will also allow for audit and control.

The Balanced Scorecard: Explanation and Application

The *Balanced Scorecard* is a tool that allows us to manage knowledge, boost international strategy, corporate culture and control mechanisms and to evolve in this through the use of technology.

❝You must have learned about the Balanced Scorecard. I use it at Microsoft International, across 105 international subs worldwide: and guess what – it really works!❞

(Jean-Philippe Courtois, President of Microsoft International, Senior Vice President of Microsoft Corp. CERAM management conference, Sephia Antipolis, 3rd December 2007)

The *Balanced Scorecard* uses a top-down approach to business performance management. It extracts business strategic intent and moves this down through the organization to operational core entities. The focus of the *Balanced Scorecard* is its link and/or influences between its various components, which include business strategy, perspectives, objectives, measures, initiatives and milestones as well as contextual information. At the same time, it develops and transfers essential knowledge in the company context.

In **financials**, the Balanced Scorecard examines the shareholder perception of the company, most often separated into short-term and long-term objectives. Further parts of the scorecard examine other measures (revenue, growth rate, return on assets, turnover rate), targets (commercial targets and growth targets) and initiatives (increase in production, productivity, sales management programmes, intensive distribution). This information complements financial scores with those stemming from **non-financial measures** (speed of response, product quality; external factors such as customer satisfaction, brand preference; forward-looking measures, such as idea management and employee satisfaction). Management defines these measures and enables its people to learn what works best in the organization, and to develop, transfer and control knowledge.

Remember: All objectives on the scorecard are related to the business life cycle specific to the firm. Its aim is to sustain growth, stability, measure ROE

(Return on Equity), ROCE (Return on Capital Employed), EVA (Earned Value Analysis), harvest strong financial policies through the control of financial income, cash flow and cash dividend ration through financial and non-financial means.

Taking it **FURTHER**

In particular, the Anglo-Saxon business model focuses on the importance of shareholder wealth as a primary business objective. In this, business that improves shareholder satisfaction will quasi-automatically increase stakeholder satisfaction in the long term. This does not exclude a certain interest in other stakeholders. The stakeholder model stipulates that responsibilities of the company go further than its shareholders, to a wider group: that is, one of the goals of the company is its responsibility to a given range of stakeholders, as well as the perception of manager responsibilities within this. Therefore, it can be stated rather simply that a stakeholder company is a company that deems itself responsible in terms of shareholders as well as any other group (customers, governmental and non-governmental actors, communities and infrastructures). This concept has strong advocates in Europe.

The *Balanced Scorecard* also helps companies determine which customers to serve and in which market segments to primarily compete, as a main source of revenue that serves the firm's financial objectives (measured by market share, customer retention – rate at which a business unit maintains ongoing relationships with its customers, customer acquisition, customer satisfaction – the satisfaction level of customers along specific performance criteria within the value proposition, customer profitability – the net profit of a customer after allowing for the unique expenses required to support that customer). The scorecard helps extract the essential factors that develop, sustain and potentially improve its performance.

Ultimately, the scorecard is used to improve and monitor the internal business process: it shows the performance of business and its entities, its regions and subsidiaries, products and service segments vis-à-vis the mission announced. These may be:

- mission-oriented processes: specific functions of offices or entities that may show unique challenges
- support processes: these are repetitive in nature, straightforward and easy to measure and benchmark by use of generic metrics.

To maintain a *comparative advantage*, international companies strive to reduce cost, improve quality and life cycle times, reduce duplication of efforts and increase yields. Knowledge management tools help here, with a clear learning and growth perspective.

The scorecard includes employee training and corporate cultural attitudes related to individual and corporate self-improvement: with the complexity and speed of international business and technological change, knowledge workers are an essential resource and need continuous, employee-centred learning, with a measure of time to process maturity, and that of time to market (compared to that of competitors).

So-called 'Learning and Growth Perspectives' stemming from efficient KM encompass:

1 employee capability

2 employee satisfaction

3 employee retention

4 employee productivity

5 information system capabilities

6 motivation, empowerment and alignment.

KM is therefore a people-oriented management tool that is of particular use for international business with its enlarged market and organizational base, its diversity and its – often broad – business and organizational objectives. It develops, adapts, manages and controls what managers and entities know and perceive, and human competency, intuition, ideas and motivations can be linked effectively to the corporate culture, mission and goals. KM is strongly supported by technology but humanly defined and run.

The main change conditions that increase the need for sound KM are:

* increasingly international competition
* streamlined sectors and industries
* an increasing rate, rhythm and diffusion of innovation

- cost and staff reductions (due to competitive pressure and a reduction of time allocated to training/learning) – these drive the need to transform informal, tacit knowledge into formal, explicit knowledge
- demographic change, ageing populations, retirements and the increasing international mobility of labour – these all add new challenges to KM.

What is the basic need and motivation for good KM?

Good KM is hence dependent on good leadership – awareness-raising throughout the firm can boost reputation-building externally, and it ideally internodes business processes and practices into:

- *change management*, project management
- best practices, benchmarking, quality management
- risk management
- outsourcing and other management issues.

'What applications of KM take place in fields such as Project Management, Quality Management, outsourcing and other management issues?'

Quality Management

Rugman et al., 2006, note that international companies prioritize locations using the criteria of local market requirements and resources, including local knowledge and so-called *national systems of innovation* and quality. In a systematic and more effective way, quality management can be improved, among many other fields. Its applications, of course, vary depending on the company, business sector and industry. In manufacturing, this can concern, the following:

- The record of quality standards and procedures: many working quality standards and procedures can be recorded in paper form and/or electronic files. These documents should be easily accessible and presented clearly at the workplace in order to increase the quality awareness of the operators. Furthermore, the documents are good sources for employee quality training programmes, and team meetings.
- The record of tacit know-how: much quality problem-solving know-how is inherent in team leaders and their teams. It should be transferred from tacit knowledge, for example of operators, to an explicit knowledge or documented knowledge in paper form and/or electronic files. Many companies set up databases to

gather this know-how, quality problem-solving, and quality judgement criteria, to create a knowledge base for the organization.

- The distribution of lessons learnt: in Japanese manufacturing companies, the diffusion of quality lessons learnt is a way to let operators know, understand and learn from past quality problems. With this method, organizations and people learn from experience and prevent the same quality problems from re-occuring.

Project Management

Knowledge Management helps in achieving project completion and excellence. Projects vary in terms of size, teams, duration, objectives and stakeholders. Nonetheless, in an organization, components, processes, information and expertise are ideally shared across projects or are repeatedly utilized from one project to another. This is only possible when knowledge is extracted, processed and transferred about the project and these components, on a platform on which a given project team can learn from 'already existing' knowledge and perform in an efficient, effective and consistent manner. While this boosts performance and cuts costs, it also adds value to the team, its achievements and hence its motivation, making it more profitable and productive. Here is a sample list of the many benefits that good KM can bring about. It can:

- minimize the redundancy of information,
- increase knowledge sharing: using a library of best practices and previous knowledge or repeated tasks, and knowing the structure of how to accomplish them, the project team will utilize its time in more productive activities and goals, rather than trying to accomplish redundant tasks which have been completed before. This includes note-taking processes and procedures and resources that could be used in future projects.
- provide specialized experts in each project area. These experts need not be assigned full-time to each project. The key here is to draw upon the knowledge of these experts from time to time and to make them available when they are needed. They need to have the knowledge of the team's evolution to the date of intervention, while the team needs to know which expert can contribute what value.
- provide expert knowledge in similar scenarios that can be kept as a repository and duplicated across projects. But it must be effectively structured, with defined boundaries and limitations. Each participant must understand how to effectively utilize the knowledge, and they must be trained in extracting the right knowledge or being able to look for additional resources with a structured approach. With best practice achieving the removal of redundancy, the team will ideally be more productive and valuable, and hence the project will be driven according to specifications and achieve profitability and on-time completion.

Outsourcing and other Management Issues

In the context of outsourcing (transfer of services to a third party), KM becomes a challenge, in terms of the development of knowledge and for its transfer. Outsourcing is normally motivated by firms seeking to enhance their competitive advantage through:

- low costs (*economies of scale*)
- access to knowledge and resources
- the focus of fully-employed staff on core competencies
- diversifying risks from peripheral competencies
- a lack of in-house resources
- in-house or external efficiencies or effectiveness
- systems of innovation
- network advantages
- increased in-house commercial flexibility
- tighter budget control through predictability of costs (this frees cash flow)
- lower investment in internal infrastructure.

However, at the same time, the firm may lose knowledge (in particular, newly developed knowledge) if it does not engage in a KM that encompasses its partners. Other challenges are the (partial or complete) loss of control, a distinction from competitors, the streamlining of processes to avoid redundancies, talents, a focus on the customer instead of on the product, sometimes reputation, and often also the motivation of the in-house workforce (due to the social consequences of outsourcing).

KM in these circumstances is difficult because of a divergence of interests. On the one hand, the client is seeking service, risk-sharing, and a cutting of costs and responsibilities, often at lower costs than would be the case 'in-house'. On the other hand, the vendor, mainly seeks profit, and often also reputation. The common ground may be an investment carefully designed to enhance both parties':

- capabilities
- internationalization
- agility and profitability
- competitive advantage.

Because each partner is part of a value chain that constructs an ecosystem for the vendor, cross-organizational KM needs to capture external knowledge and transfer experience made externally to management. International business is increasingly networked and 'virtual', and adapts its knowledge flows and externalization of technologies and competencies in an adaptive manner, shifting the needs and capabilities of the partners along this value chain. When knowledge, or even KM itself, is outsourced, security concerns become relevant. Often, project management, application development and testing remain in-house when IT and/or KM are outsourced so as to keep a handle on it.

Change Management and KM

In *change management*, KM helps develop, utilize and transfer the process, tools and techniques that help individuals make successful career transitions which result in awareness of a need for change and its adoption.

"People get very concerned and worked up about whether they'll have a job and what that job will be. The sooner people know, the less turmoil you have."

(Lord Colin Marshal of Knightsbridge, Chairman, British Airways CNN money, 1988)

Internally, management interacts with employees at all levels within the organization when a change takes place, and needs to raise this awareness and adoption mechanism so as to retain its talents and competencies. Planning for change is followed by its management of change and its reinforcing and control. This typically happens through:

- individual change models and propositions
- communications (direct and indirect)
- sponsorship, coaching, training and mentoring
- resistance management.

Exam question: Can management use a 'one-fits-all' approach in times of organizational change or repositioning? At the beginning, management assesses the organization's change readiness, in all locations, and develops a change management strategy that might be standardized to some extent, but may need to adapt to local realities and needs in some locations due to a diversity of business environments, labour laws and conditions, and cultural assimilation. Identify and prepare the change management resources. The leadership will then determine and prepare executive sponsors, who communicate, create and manage the change management plans. Audit compliance and design methods to reinforce the change in the organization including activities to celebrate success, but also take reasonable transition periods into account that may, here again, vary from one location to another due to inherent conditions there. The aim is that change is created in the management activities of the day-to-day business manager, and that the staff's motivation and productivity are retained.

A project team, senior corporate leaders, managers, supervisors, and employees are hence the main actors in *change management*. They need to share knowledge that is based on past and present experience, clear and timely communication, and a full understanding of the desired change and the corporate mission. Externally, this communication and *change management* primarily concern direct stakeholders that include suppliers, customers, partners, investors, banks, governments and communities.

For example, internationalization requires change in the internal and external environments of the firm. Staff and managers may be required to learn new skills, possibly adopt a new corporate or international culture, and accept new missions, projects, priorities and measures of success. Individuals at different levels of the company need an understanding of the needs and motivation for this change, the impact on oneself, one's team and the company, the engagement that is needed and expected from the individual, the team and the organization, and the preparation required.

"In general, successful transformations require 70–90% leadership vs. 10–30% management effort."

(Army Business Transformation Center, www.army.mil, January 2008)

For all stakeholders in change, informal and indirect relationships are used to transfer change variables and knowledge, so that influence (one of KM's goals – see above!) can be exercised and change can be adopted. This will use skills such as learning and reward, and infrastructures with a 'road map' or a 'blueprint' of change that is communicated directly and indirectly, through conferences, seminars, meetings, the intranet, groupware, etc., and enabled by leadership.

'Does KM raise any questions of ethics and sustainable development?'

Surely KM also raises these questions, in particular because we deal with a focus on human input and the processing of data and information into knowledge that is subject to judgement, value and beliefs. This may concern issues dealing with information quality, reliability, access, confidentiality, diffusion and behaviour in the cyber-community, the status of direct and indirect actors, and responsibility and risk. A deontology (good business conduct) for one may not be the same for another (that for a journalist is not necessarily that of a programme designer that is not necessarily that of a corporate leader), and codes or charts of ethics and conducts (for example that of Bill Gates) are not accepted or acceptable universally. In any circumstances, only knowledge that is perceived as quality and trustworthy will lead to an opportunity and a decision to the benefit of a company. The challenges are high for international corporations operating under high degrees of diversity, and striving for competitive intelligence.

Recommended reading

CZINKOTA ET AL. (2005), *Part 5, Chapter 10*
RUGMAN ET AL. (2006), *Chapter 10*
BARTLETT ET AL. (2003), *p. 484*

2.11

the international economy and international trade *or*: why and how is international business influenced by the global policy environment?

❝The process by which the economic relations between nations tend to intensify at intervals faster than the economic relations domestically (inside the nation)❞

(Dictionnaire de L'Economie/Economics Dictionary.
Larousse/HER, 2000, p. 338)

In section 2.2, we reviewed the main theories that help us understand, in economic theory, why countries trade with one another, and why firms go abroad. Section 2.6 provided you with the internationalization tools, that is, the manners and means to go abroad.

The international economy is more and more globalized and integrated. This is why firms can exploit advantages internationally and outperform domestic-only business. Also, this is why trade relations between countries are stimulated, which again boosts trade and investments among their firms. The political economy sustains these phenomena. This section deals with the way in which the political economy works and in which international governmental and non-governmental institutions are involved in the regulation of it, and of international business.

The political economy and international business

The political economy deals with issues covering the many areas of:

- *monetary theory*
- *fiscal policy*
- labour economics
- planning and development
- micro- and macro-economic theory
- international trade and finance
- industrial organization
- and their interconnection.

The political economy spans into disciplines of the history of economic thought, geopolitics and social economics. Studies of the political economy were forwarded from Aristotle to Jean Jacques Rousseau to John Stuart Mill and many other thinkers who were not primarily economists or management researchers. The way in which the above-cited issues evolve goes hand in hand with the state of economics and politics, and its developments and linkages. That means that the political economy is not static but evolves continuously. The political economy can be analysed as that of a state, region or international authority. For example, the impact of financial crisis on economic growth and its consequences for business cycles and governmental control policies are part of the political economy.

In this, international institutions may play a role, for example, resolving trade disputes, regulating trade issues, or providing incentives for cooperation instead of conflict on an economic and/or geopolitical level.

International institutions: what's their use in international business, and who are they?

A range of international institutions play a role in the shaping of the international business environment. Trade and investment issues in international business reach further than the domestic authority can typically handle. They can involve bilateral trade disputes, or international harmonization efforts or many types of crises that have to be dealt with by more than one or two national authorities. Also, some national authorities do not wish to deal directly with one another: international institutions then provide an opportunity to get round a negotiation table with mediation by a neutral party. Finally, international *non-governmental organizations (NGOs)* monitor political and economic environments through many different lenses and perspectives (e.g. that of consumer protection, that of business associations, or that of human rights). Their role is important because they can intervene differently than governmental organizations; many of them provide a transparency to business, explore good and bad practices of corporations and other actors in the business environment, and are often less prone to administrative red tape.

> The United Nations Framework Convention on Climate Change, signed by more than 180 countries as the 'Bali roadmap' in December 2007, sets targets for environmental protection and structures international efforts, and is preparing a 2012 international agreement on climate change. The World Economic Forum (an NGO) analyses and discusses the impact of global warming on international business, e.g. on food prices, water scarcity issues and conflict that bring risks and uncertainties to international business. The audience is a mix of business and political leaders, academia and civil society. Proposals elaborated at the annual meeting in Davos can feed into G8 meetings.

In the field of international organizations, the list of intergovernmental international institutions and NGOs is long.

These organisations have a great impact on the factors and condition in international business. Companies' business environment is influenced by the activities and decisions of these organizations, and a number of firms entertain partnerships with them, and make their voice and experience known. Some of the major institutions are introduced below. You will come across all of these in your international business studies.

Some of these institutions are mentioned explicitly in the main IB textbooks, but most of them are not defined. Lecturers expect you to be familiar with them, from earlier education or general knowledge, so you are well advised to read the following part and remember it well.

The United Nations (UN)

With more than 192 members, this federal global organization has been growing since its creation in 1945. Its members share six main values that are noted in its Charter: that is, freedom, equity and solidarity, tolerance, non-violence, respect for nature, and shared responsibility. The United Nations and its offices, programmes and funds work on numerous initiatives to 'make the world a better place', through conflict prevention, arms reduction, smarter sanctions, economic development, peacekeeping, environmental protection, health and food, international law and justice. For example, its International Court of Justice (in The Hague) advises on and judges cases of dispute among countries if the countries voluntarily seek this out.

The International Monetary Fund, the World Bank and 13 independent organizations (termed 'specialized agencies') are linked to the UN through cooperative agreements. They include, for example, UNCTAD (economics, trade, development), UNESCO (education, science, culture), FAO (food, agriculture), ECOSOC (economy, social affairs), UNIDO (industrial development), UNEP (environment), UNDP (development programme), WHO (health); these are autonomous bodies created by intergovernmental agreement. The International Labour Organization and the Universal Postal Union were founded earlier than the UN itself.

❝[Globalization] has reduced the sense of isolation felt in much of the developing world and has given many people in the developing world access to knowledge well beyond the reach of even the wealthiest in any country a century ago.❞

(J. Stiglitz, Chief Economist and Senior Vice-President of the World Bank, 1997–2000 and recipient of the 2001 Nobel Prize in Economics. *Globalization and its Discontents, 2002)*

The World Bank

The World Bank (see above) provides financial and technical assistance to developing countries. It consists of two institutions, the International Bank for Reconstruction and Development (IBRD) and the International Development Association (IDA), which are owned by its 185 member countries. Their aim is that of global poverty reduction and an improvement of living standards, with the IBRD serving middle-income and 'credit-worthy', poor countries. The IDA's objective is to help the least developed countries in the world. The institutions provide low-interest loans, interest-free credit and grants that are mainly to serve education, health, infrastructure, communications, and work hand in hand with NGOs and other partners.

"As informed and effective advocates, non-governmental organizations (NGOs) have had a role in shaping the GEF [Global Environment Facility of the World Bank] and its agenda from the beginning. Today, participation by NGOs, both local and international, is crucial, not only at the project level but also in GEF policy dimensions. Village organizations and other community-based groups, academic institutions, and foundations are among the NGO partners integral to GEF's efforts. More than 150 GEF-financed projects are executed or co-executed by, or contain contracts or subcontracts to, non-governmental groups."

(www.gefweb.org/interior.aspx?id=212#id=114)

The Organization for Security and Co-operation in Europe (OSCE)

This organization consists of 55 members aiming for an international discussion on the defence of human and minority rights. This happens through politico-military, economic and environmental initiatives and its Human Dimension. Its initiatives span from democratic institution-building, to education, to the combat of terrorism and to missions that defuse ethnic and political tension.

"Freedom of investment is a core value of the OECD."

(OECD work on preventing investment protectionism, www.oecd.org, OECD, 2008)

Its decisions are only politically binding. This is the largest regional security organization in the world. Companies are encouraged to engage in good practices in these fields. Also, firms are part of the organization's tenders.

The North Atlantic Treaty Organisation (NATO)

This is an alliance among 26 countries from North America and Europe that aim to coordinate defence, security and the inviolability of frontiers. The alliance aims to guard freedom and security for its members, on the basis of the shared values of democracy, liberty, the rule of law and dispute resolution. Companies engage in business opportunities along with NATO through biddings, tenders and consultations. They are indirectly benefit from NATO through peace and stability, a major encouragement and safeguard for trade.

G7/G8

The G7/G8 is an annual meeting that deals with the macro-economic issues of its members and the larger international community. It was launched in 1975, and unites the heads of state or government of the major industrial democracies. Members are France, the United States, Britain, Germany, Japan and Italy (the founding countries or Group of 6/G6), joined by Canada, the European Community (G7), and Russia (G8).

The World Trade Organization (WTO)

This organization focuses on international decision-making in trade liberalization, and engages in negotiations of trade agreements and trade dispute settlement. Its 181 members use this negotiation forum for agreements that constitute most of the basis of international trade and international business. Therefore, WTO activities directly influence corporate activity.

The WTO was founded in 1995, but is an evolution of the General Agreement of Tariffs and Trade (GATT) that has grown since 1948 through rounds of negotiation, in which agreements on goods were mainly dealt with. The WTO also expanded its field to services and intellectual property issues.

*For research in this field, you are well advised to look into the following organizations' activities and databases. For example, at the **World Trade Organization (WTO)** website, extensive information on worldwide import and export statistics is provided, mainly free of charge (www.wto.org). The **International Trade Center (ITC)** offers information files separated by individual countries; age of data depends on the selected country, but is fairly recent. Information such as trade performance indexes, national export performance, import profiles and even statistic reliability for the figures is provided. Most of the content is also free of charge (www.intracen.org). The **Federation of International Trade Associations (FITA)**, with some of the content payable, gives many useful links, including business directories, cultural information on different countries, links to glossaries and dictionaries, lists of government and multinational organizations, and several forums for trading information and more (www.fita.org).*

More international institutions contribute to the development of the international business environment. Their impact is often closely related to geopolitics, and differs depending on the economic wealth of countries and regions.

The impact of geopolitics on the political economy

In developed countries, the political economy is strongly governed and influenced by international institutions and organizations. Most of these were founded by highly developed countries with mature markets and business structures. The evolution of geopolitics is studied when one analyses power and politics in the world, and the way in which these forces interact. Each country, region or state is characterized by its geographical realities, and also by the culture and identity of its people, its history, and its capacities in many aspects, among them intelligence and military considerations. Geopolitics studies shed light on conflict and cooperation in the world. International trade and the risks and benefits of doing business internationally rely on geopolitics that, in the best case for the firm, show a tradition of stability and welfare in the civil society.

Rugman et al., 2006, for example, define the civil society (or: wider community) as 'a group of individuals, organisations and institutions that act outside the government and the market to advance a diverse set of interests' (p. 111).

In this case, firms can confidently invest in such an area; indeed, international investments are higher in regions of geopolitical stability. Following the theories explained in the earlier sections, this is very beneficial for business and the civil society. Many international governmental and non-governmental organizations aim for an increase in cooperation (on different levels, e.g. political or economic) and the decrease of dispute, conflict and crisis.

Why does this have an impact on business?

In this, business is mainly concerned with the effects of *free trade* and protectionism that may govern the political economy internationally and in particular markets.

Typically, stability boosts trade relations that increase corporate efficiency and improve economic performance. Firms integrate international activities to improve profitability. This works depending on the strategic response that management can provide to changes in the business environment, threats, opportunities, and decreasing or increasing stability.

Some changes however may be negatively related to geopolitics, for example in the shape of trade barriers, *trade sanctions* and *embargoes*.

Countries and trade blocs may favour protectionism to *free trade*, for different reasons. Protecting their domestic industries means that foreign trade is limited. These trade barriers cause constraints to international business, typically on both sides of the trade balance, because trade partners may retaliate at protectionist behaviours by imposing restrictions too. This raises the costs and diminishes competitive advantages, and may cause companies to set up operations elsewhere. A firm will optimally strive to be part of the 'in-group' and not to suffer from trade barriers. If those barriers give cause to trade disputes, international organizations such as the WTO can be asked to take position and help in their resolution.

Trade sanctions are different. These are trade penalties that countries impose against others.

Sanctions were imposed by a number of countries against Burma in 2008 due to the governmental repression of the opposition demanding more democracy and freedom. Among them, the USA prohibited new investment in Burma by US persons, as well as US persons' facilitation of new investment in Burma by foreign persons. The USA restricted funds and property, and the exportation of financial services to Burma. The Office of Foreign Assets Control of the US Treasury administers sanctions against 'Libya, Cuba, North Korea, Iran, Iraq, Syria, Sudan, Zimbabwe, Liberia, certain targets in the Western Balkans, highly enriched uranium transactions, diamond trading, designated terrorists and international narcotics traffickers, Foreign Terrorist

> Organizations, and designated foreign persons who have engaged in activities relating to the proliferation of weapons of mass destruction'
> (www.ustreas.gov/offices/enforcement/ofac/programs/ascii/burma.txt).

Trade sanctions are hence used to influence actors in the international community when a particular event or issue causes concern for stability. *Embargoes* prohibit the supply of goods or service, such as arms or equipment to certain countries. This ban can concern imports, exports and all trade of specific products or services. The objective is the isolation, pressure and ultimately the reversal of a given policy that a country, an organization, or a group engages in.

> Osama bin Laden, the Al-Qaida network and the Taliban are the aim of the arms embargo installed by UN Security Council Resolution 1390 (16 January 2002).

Import embargoes put a strain on the domestic economy in the country/-ies that impose them, because supply falls, prices rise and alternatives have to be found. When exports are embargoed, the opposite effect (rising supply) can lead to very low prices and pose major problems to production, possibly even leading to layoffs.

Otherwise, controls of international business focus mainly on military and dual-use goods and services (the latter may be technology or software that can be used for civil and military purposes). The European Union (EU), just like many other market authorities, has ratified specific legislation that focuses on these issues and lists sensitive products and services. An export license system exists that can authorize export under certain conditions and a code of conduct.

Taking it **FURTHER**

Do not mix up trade sanctions and embargoes with boycotts. Boycotts are voluntary retreats from engaging in some type of partnership or commercial practice with a party that is perceived as doing wrong. For example, Mahatma Gandhi called for a boycott against British goods in December 1921 for protest reasons. Boycotts are mainly used for awareness-raising about issues perceived as unethical. NGOs play a significant role through the observation of the normally ethical conduct of, for example, international companies. They can be at the origin of product or company boycotts to fight against child labour, sweatshops or tests on animals.

Some changes in international affairs are positive, and create business opportunities, for example in market groupings. Also, the success of economic integration is due to well-developed productive forces and well-developed market relations between countries that are stable.

In less-developed countries (LDCs), stability and economic relations help develop intragroup trade, in a need for development per se, because foreign trade is usually large relative to domestic production. Stability and dispute settlement are often dependent on external help from organizations that rationalize the emerging structure of production and increase the opportunities for profitable investment by domestic and foreign firms, at its best stimulating the production of import substitutes.

'Does globalization influence the role of international organizations and NGOS? How and why?'

Challenges such as environmental issues, ethical concerns, international risk dimensions and geopolitical conflict reach further than national boundaries. The same goes for the analysis that a company needs to make of the political economy that it is exposed to. The many issues and challenges that may impede fair international trade, in which reciprocity should underpin the interests of parties to deal with each other, are regulated by international institutions. These institutions therefore gain power at the same time as globalization opens more and more markets, and increases exchanges on an international scale.

These institutions can only function when national authorities respect their functioning and judgment. For this, national authorities give up some sovereignty and power, because they agree that decisions can be made by other institutions (e.g. the UN or the WTO) and need to be applied. NGOs increase companies' and governments' awareness of issues that have to be solved, or of issues that attract wide attention in the civil society and may have an impact on growth and value creation.

International business benefits companies and economies. It has developed through the opening of trade, and also on the basis of ambitions of nations, corporations, states and international finance. This is reinforced by the demands of consumers for low-cost products, high-quality service, and the rapid and seemingly never-ending possibilities stemming from technology. International business can also put strains on communities and identities to be preserved, on prices and commodities, on the natural environment, the quality of life of communities and ethical behaviour. International business has a major role to play in our societies, and needs to be aware of and responsible for this role. Institutions and international organizations are there to help structure this role for the benefit of all, if possible. Global regulatory institutions, for example the World Trade Organization, International Monetary Fund and World Bank are indispensable actors in international economic and political relations.

Recommended reading

CZINKOTA ET AL. **(2005),** *Chapters 11 and 19*
RUGMAN AND HODGETTS: **(1995)** *Chapter 12*
HILL **(2008),** *Chapter 4*

Introduction

If you work your way carefully through this section, you should by the
end be better equipped to profit from your lectures, benefit from your
seminars, construct your essays efficiently, develop effective revision
strategies and respond comprehensively to the pressures of exam situations. In the five sections that lie ahead, you will be presented with:
checklists and bullet points to focus your attention on key issues; exercises to help you participate actively in the learning experience; illustrations and analogies to enable you to anchor learning principles in
everyday events and experiences; worked examples to demonstrate the
use of such features as structure, headings and continuity; and tips that
provide practical advice in a nutshell form.

In the exercises that are presented, each student should decide how
much effort they would like to invest in each exercise, according to individual preferences and requirements. Some of the points in the exercises
will be covered in the text either before or after the exercise. You might
prefer to read each section right through before going back to tackle the
exercises. Suggested answers are provided in italics after some of the exercises, so avoid these if you would prefer to work through the exercises on
your own. The aim is to prompt you to reflect on the material, remember what you have read and trigger you to add your own thoughts. Space
is provided for you to write your responses down in a few words, or you
may prefer to reflect on them within your own mind. However, writing
will help you to slow down and digest the material and may also enable
you to process the information at a deeper level of learning.

Finally, the overall aim of the section is to point you to the keys for
academic and personal development. The twin emphases of academic
development and personal qualities are stressed throughout. By giving
attention to these factors, you will give yourself the toolkit you will
need to excel in your studies.

*in collaboration with David McIlroy

3.1	
how to get the most out of your lectures	

This section will show you how to:

- make the most of your lecture notes
- prepare your mind for new terms
- develop an independent approach to learning
- write efficient summary notes from lectures
- take the initiative in building on your lectures.

Keeping in context

According to higher educational commentators and advisors, the best quality learning is facilitated when it is set within an overall learning context. It should be the responsibility of your tutors to provide a context for you to learn in, but it is your responsibility to see this overall context, and you can do this even before your first lecture begins. Such a panoramic view can be achieved by becoming familiar with the outline content of both a given subject and the entire study programme. Before you go into each lecture, you should briefly remind yourself of where it fits into the overall scheme of things. Think, for example, of how more confident you feel when you move to a new city (e.g. to attend university) once you become familiar with your bearings – i.e. where you live in relation to college, shops, stores, buses, trains, places of entertainment, etc.

> *The same principle applies to your course – find your way around your study programme and locate the position of each lecture within this overall framework.*

Use of lecture notes

It is always beneficial to do some preliminary reading before you enter a lecture. If lecture notes are provided in advance (e.g. electronically), then print these out, read over them and bring them with you to the lecture. You can insert question marks on issues where you will need further clarification. Some lecturers prefer to provide full notes, some prefer to make skeleton outlines available and some prefer to issue no notes at all! If notes are provided, take full advantage and supplement these with your own notes as you listen. In a later section on memory techniques, you will see that humans possess the ability to 're-learn savings', i.e. it is easier to learn material the second time around, as it is evident that we have a capacity to hold residual memory deposits. So some basic preparation will equip you with a great advantage – you will be able to 'tune in' and think more clearly about the lecture than you would have done with the preliminary work.

If you set yourself too many tedious tasks at the early stages of your academic programme, you may lose some motivation and momentum. A series of short, simple, achievable tasks can give your mind the 'lubrication' you need. For example, you are more likely to maintain preliminary reading for a lecture if you set modest targets.

Mastering technical terms

Let us assume that in an early lecture you are introduced to a series of new terms such as 'paradigm' or 'empirical'. If you are hearing these and other terms for the first time, you could end up with a headache! New words can be threatening, especially if you have to face a string of them in one lecture. The uncertainty about the new terms may impair your ability to benefit fully from the lecture and therefore hinder the quality of your learning. Some subjects require technical terms and the use of them is unavoidable. However, when you have heard a term a number of times, it will not seem as daunting as it initially was. It is claimed that individuals may have particular strengths in the scope of their vocabulary. Some people may have a good recognition vocabulary – they immediately know what a word means when they read it or hear it in context. Others have a good command of language when they speak – they have an ability to recall words freely. Still others are more fluent in recall when they write – words seem to flow rapidly for them when they engage in the dynamics of writing. You can work at developing all three approaches in your course, and the checklist below the next paragraph may be of some help in mastering and marshalling the terms you hear in lectures.

In terms of learning new words, it will be very useful if you can first try to work out what they mean from their context when you first encounter them. You might be much better at this than you imagine, especially if there is only one word in the sentence that you do not understand. It would also be very useful if you could obtain a small indexed notebook and use this to build up your own glossary of terms. In this way, you could include a definition of a word, an example of its use, where it fits into a theory and any practical application of it.

Checklist for mastering terms used in your lectures

✓ Read your lecture notes before the lectures and list any unfamiliar terms.

✓ Read over the listed terms until you are familiar with their sound.

✓ Try to work out the meanings of terms from their context.

✓ Do not suspend the learning of the meaning of a term indefinitely.

✓ Write out a sentence that includes the new word (do this for each word).

✓ Meet with other students and test each other with the technical terms.

✓ Jot down new words you hear in lectures and check out the meaning soon afterwards.

> *Your confidence will greatly increase when you begin to follow the flow of arguments that contain technical terms, and more especially when you can freely use the terms yourself in speaking and writing.*

Developing independent study

In the current educational ethos, there are the twin aims of cultivating teamwork/group activities and independent learning. There is not necessarily a conflict between the two, as they should complement each other. For example, if you are committed to independent learning, you have more to offer other students when you work in small groups, and you will also be prompted to follow up on the leads given by them. Furthermore, the guidelines given to you in lectures are designed to lead you into deeper independent study. The issues raised in lectures are pointers to provide direction and structure for your extended personal pursuit. Your aim should invariably be to build on what you are given, and you should never think of merely returning the bare bones of the lecture material in a course-work essay or exam.

> *It is always very refreshing to a marker to be given work from a student that contains recent studies that the examiner had not previously encountered.*

Note-taking strategy

Note-taking in lectures is an art that you will only perfect with practice and by trial and error. Each student should find the formula that works best for him or her. What works for one does not necessarily work for another. Some students can write more quickly than others, some are better at shorthand than others and some are better at deciphering their own scrawl! The problem will always be to try to find a balance between concentrating beneficially on what you hear and making sufficient notes that will enable you to comprehend what you have heard later. You should not however become frustrated by the fact that you will not understand or remember immediately everything you have heard.

> *By being present at a lecture, and by making some attempt to attend to what you hear, you will already have a substantial advantage over those students who do not attend.*

Guidelines for note-taking in lectures

- Develop the note-taking strategy that works best for you.
- Work at finding a balance between listening and writing.
- Make some use of optimal shorthand (e.g. a few key words may summarize a story).
- Too much writing may impair the flow of the lecture for you.
- Too much writing may impair the quality of your notes.
- Some limited notes are better than none.
- Good note-taking may facilitate a deeper processing of information.
- It is essential to 'tidy up' notes as soon as possible after a lecture.
- Reading over notes soon after lectures will consolidate your learning.

Developing the lecture

Some educationalists have criticized the value of lectures because they allege that these are merely a mode of 'passive learning'. This can certainly be an accurate conclusion to arrive at (that is, if students approach lectures in the wrong way) and lecturers can work to devise ways of making lectures more interactive. For example, they can make use of interactive handouts or by posing questions during the lecture and giving time out for students to reflect on these. Other possibilities are short discussions at given junctures in the lecture or the use of small groups within the session. As a student, you do not have to enter a lecture in passive mode and you can ensure that you are not merely a passive recipient of information by taking steps to develop the lecture yourself. A list of suggestions is presented below to help you take the initiative in developing the lecture content.

Checklist to ensure that the lecture is not merely a passive experience

✓ Try to interact with the lecture material by asking questions.

✓ Highlight points that you would like to develop in personal study.

✓ Trace connections between the lecture and other parts of your study programme.

✓ Bring together notes from the lecture and other sources.

✓ Restructure the lecture outline into your own preferred format.

✓ Think of ways in which aspects of the lecture material can be applied.

✓ Design ways in which aspects of the lecture material can be illustrated.

✓ If the lecturer invites questions, make a note of all the questions asked.

✓ Follow up on issues of interest that have arisen out of the lecture.

> *You can contribute to this active involvement in a lecture by engaging with the material before, during and after it is delivered.*

EXERCISE

Checklist – You might now like to attempt to summarize (and/or add) some factors that would help you to capitalize fully on the benefits of a lecture:

✓ ....

✓ ....

✓ ....

✓ ....

✓ ....

3.2

how to make the most of seminars

This section will show you how to:

- be aware of the value of seminars
- focus on links to learning
- recognize qualities you can use repeatedly
- manage potential problems in seminars
- prepare yourself adequately for seminars.

Not to be underestimated

Seminars are often optional in a degree programme and sometimes poorly attended because they are underestimated. Some students may be convinced that the lecture is the truly authoritative way to receive quality information. Undoubtedly, lectures play an important role in an academic programme, but seminars have a unique contribution to learning that will complement lectures. Other students may feel that their time would be better spent in personal study. Again, private study is unquestionably essential for personal learning and development, but you will nevertheless diminish your learning experience if you neglect seminars. If seminars were to be removed from academic programmes, then something really important would be lost.

Checklist – Some useful features of seminars

They:

- ✓ can identify problems that you had not thought of
- ✓ can clear up confusing issues
- ✓ allow you to ask questions and make comments
- ✓ can help you develop friendships and teamwork
- ✓ enable you to refresh and consolidate your knowledge
- ✓ can help you sharpen motivation and redirect study efforts.

An asset to complement other learning activities

In higher education at the present time, there is an emphasis on variety – variety in delivery, learning experience, learning styles and assessment methods. The seminar is deemed to hold an important place within the overall scheme of teaching, learning and assessment. In some programmes, the seminars are directly linked to the assessment task. Whether or not they have such a place in your course, they will provide you with a unique opportunity to learn and develop.

In a seminar, you will hear a variety of contributions, and different perspectives and emphases. You will have the chance to interrupt and the experience of being interrupted! You will also learn that you can get things wrong and still survive! It is often the case that when one student admits that they did not know some important piece of information, other students quickly follow with the same admission in the wake of this. If you can learn to ask questions and not feel stupid, then seminars will give you an asset for learning and a lifelong educational quality.

Creating the right climate in seminars

It has been said that we have been given only one mouth to talk, but two ears to listen. One potential problem with seminars is that some students may take a while to learn this lesson, and other students may have to help hasten them on the way (graciously but firmly!). In lectures, your main role is to listen and take notes, but in seminars there is the challenge to strike the balance between listening and speaking. It is important to make a beginning in speaking even if it is just to repeat something that you agree with. You can also learn to disagree in an agreeable way. For example, you can raise a question against what someone else has said and pose this in a good way – e.g. 'If that is the case, does that not mean that ...'. In addition, it is perfectly possible to disagree with others by avoiding personal attacks, such as, 'that was a really stupid thing to say', or 'I thought you knew better than that', or 'I'm surprised that you don't know that by now'. Educationalists say that it is important to have the right climate to learn in, and the avoidance of unnecessary conflict will foster such a climate.

Checklist – Suggest what can be done to reach agreement (set ground rules) that would help keep seminars running smoothly and harmoniously:

✓ ....

✓ ....

✓ ....

✓ ....

✓ ....

Some suggestions are: appoint someone to guide and control the discussion, invite individuals to prepare in advance to make a contribution, hand out agreed discussion questions at some point prior to the seminar, stress at the beginning that no one should monopolize the discussion and emphasize that there must be no personal attacks on any individual (state clearly what this means). Also, you could invite and encourage quieter students to participate and assure each person that their contribution is valued.

Links in learning and transferable skills

An important principle in learning to progress from shallow to deep learning is developing the capacity to make connecting links between themes or topics and across subjects. This also applies to the various learning activities such as lectures, seminars, fieldwork, computer searches and private study. Another factor to think about is: 'what skills can I develop, or improve on, from seminars that I can use across my study programme?' A couple of examples of key skills are the ability to communicate and the capacity to work within a team. These are skills that you will be able to use at various points in your course (transferable), but you are not likely to develop them within the formal setting of a lecture.

EXERCISE

Checklist – Write out or think about (a) three things that give seminars value, and (b) three useful skills that you can develop in seminars:

(a)

✓ ....
✓ ....
✓ ....

(b)

✓ ....
✓ ....
✓ ....

In the above exercises, for (a), you could have: a variety of contributors, the flexibility to spend more time on problematic issues and an agreed agenda settled at the beginning of the seminar. For (b), you could have: communication, conflict resolution and teamwork.

A key question that you should bring to every seminar is 'How does this seminar connect with my other learning activities and my assessments?'

An opportunity to contribute

If you have never made a contribution to a seminar before, you may need something to use as an 'ice breaker'. It does not matter if your first contribution is only a sentence or two – the important thing is to make a start. One way to do this is to make brief notes as others contribute, and while doing this, a question or two might arise in your mind. If your first contribution is a question, that is a good start. Or it may be that you will be able to point out some connection between what others have said, or identify conflicting opinions that need to be resolved. If you have already begun making contributions, it is important that you keep the momentum going, and do not allow yourself to lapse back into the safe cocoon of shyness.

See if you can suggest how you might resolve some of the following problems that might hinder you from making a contribution to seminars:

- There is one student who dominates and monopolizes the discussion.
- Someone else has already said what you really want to say.
- You are afraid that someone else will correct you and make you feel stupid.
- You feel that your contribution might be seen as short and shallow.
- A previous negative experience puts you off making any more contributions.

If you are required to bring a presentation to your seminar, you might want to consult a full chapter on presentations in a complementary study guide (McIlroy, 2003). Alternatively, you may be content with the summary bullet points presented at the end of this section. In order to benefit from discussions in seminars (the focus of this section), some useful summary nutshells are now presented as a checklist.

Checklist – How to benefit from seminars

✓ Do some preparatory reading.
✓ Familiarize yourself with the main ideas to be addressed.
✓ Make notes during the seminar.
✓ Make some verbal contribution, even a question.
✓ Remind yourself of the skills you can develop.
✓ Trace learning links from the seminar to other subjects/topics on your programme.
✓ Make brief bullet points on what you should follow up on.
✓ Read over your notes as soon as possible after the seminar.
✓ Continue a discussion with fellow students after the seminar has ended.

If required to give a presentation:

- have a practice run with friends
- if using visuals, do not obstruct them
- check out beforehand that all equipment works
- space out points clearly on visuals (large and legible)
- time your talk by your visuals (e.g. five slides per 15 minute talk = three minutes per slide)

- make sure your talk synchronizes with the slide on view at any given point
- project your voice so that all in the room can hear
- inflect your voice and do not stand motionless
- spread eye contact around the audience
- avoid the twin extremes of a fixed gaze at individuals and never looking at anyone
- be aware that it is better to fall a little short of time allocation than to run over it
- be selective in what you choose to present
- map out where you are going and summarize your main points at the end.

3.3

essay writing tips

This section will show you how to:

- quickly engage with the main arguments
- channel your passions constructively
- note your main arguments in an outline
- find and focus on your central topic questions
- weave quotations into your essay.

Getting into the flow

In essay writing, one of your first aims should be to get your mind active and engaged with your subject. Tennis players like to go out onto the court and hit the ball back and forth just before the competitive match begins. This allows them to judge the bounce of the ball, feel its weight against their racket, get used to the height of the net, the parameters of the court and other factors such as temperature, light, sun and the crowd. In the same way, you can 'warm up' for your essay by tossing the ideas to and fro within your head before you begin to write. This will allow you to think within the framework of your topic, and this will be especially important if you are coming to the subject for the first time.

The tributary principle

A tributary is a stream that runs into a main river as it wends its way to the sea. Similarly, in an essay you should ensure that every idea you introduce is moving toward the overall theme you are addressing. Your idea might of course be relevant to a subheading that is in turn relevant to a main heading. Every idea you introduce is to be a 'feeder' into the flowing theme. In addition to tributaries, there can also be 'distributaries', which are streams that flow away from the river. In an essay, these would represent the ideas that run away from the main stream of thought and leave the reader trying to work out what their relevance may have been. It is one thing to have grasped your subject thoroughly, but quite another to convince your reader that this is the case. Your aim should be to build up ideas sentence by sentence and paragraph by paragraph, until you have communicated your clear purpose to the reader.

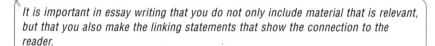

It is important in essay writing that you do not only include material that is relevant, but that you also make the linking statements that show the connection to the reader.

Listing and linking the key concepts

All subjects will have central concepts that can sometimes be usefully labelled by a single word. Course textbooks may include a glossary of terms and these provide a direct route to the beginning of an efficient mastery of the topic. The central words or terms are the essential raw materials that you will need to build upon. Ensure that you learn the words and their definitions, and that you can go on to link the key words together so that in your learning activities you will add understanding to your basic memory work.

It is useful to list your key words under general headings if that is possible and logical. You may not always see the connections immediately but when you later come back to a problem that seemed intractable, you will often find that your thinking is much clearer.

Example – Write an essay on ' The aspects and perceptions of ageing'

You might decide to draft your outline points in the following manner (or you may prefer to use a mind map approach):

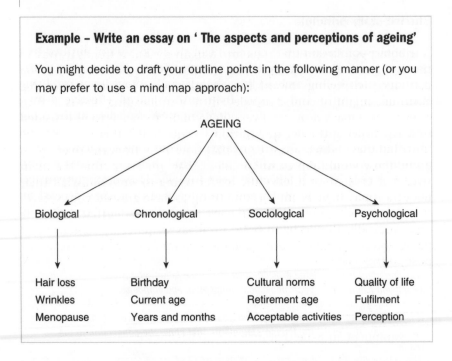

Biological	Chronological	Sociological	Psychological
Hair loss	Birthday	Cultural norms	Quality of life
Wrinkles	Current age	Retirement age	Fulfilment
Menopause	Years and months	Acceptable activities	Perception

An adversarial system

In higher education, students are required to make the transition from descriptive to critical writing. If you can think of the critical approach as like a law case that is being conducted where there is both a prosecution and a defence. Your concern should be for objectivity, transparency and fairness. No matter how passionately you may feel about a given cause, you must not allow information to be filtered out because of your personal prejudice. An essay is not to become a crusade for a cause in which the contrary arguments are not addressed in an even-handed manner. This means that you should show an awareness that opposite views are held and you should at least represent these as accurately as possible.

Your role as the writer is like that of the judge in that you must ensure that all the evidence is heard, and that nothing will compromise either party.

Stirring up passions

The above points do not of course mean that you are not entitled to a personal persuasion or to feel passionately about your subject. On the contrary, such feelings may well be a marked advantage if you can bring them under control and channel them into balanced, effective writing (see the example below). Some students may be struggling at the other end of the spectrum – being required to write about a topic that they feel quite indifferent about. As you engage with your topic and toss the ideas around in your mind, you will hopefully find that your interest is stimulated, if only at an intellectual level initially. How strongly you feel about a topic, or how much you are interested in it, may depend on whether you choose the topic yourself or whether it has been given to you as an obligatory assignment.

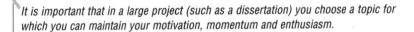

It is important that in a large project (such as a dissertation) you choose a topic for which you can maintain your motivation, momentum and enthusiasm.

An example of an issue that may stir up passions is:

Arguments for and against the existence of God

For

- The universe appears to have a design.
- Humans have an innate desire to worship.
- Humans are free to choose good or evil.
- There are common threads between religions.
- Religion provides strong moral foundations.
- Individuals report subjective experiences.
- God's revelation is in holy books.

Against

- There are flaws in the universe.
- Not all humans appear to have the desire to worship.
- How can evil be adequately explained?
- There are many religions and diverse beliefs.
- Humanists accept moral principles.
- Subjective experiences are not infallible.
- Devout people differ in interpretation.

Structuring an outline

Whenever you sense a flow of inspiration to write on a given subject, it is essential that you put this into a structure that will allow your inspiration to be communicated clearly. It is a basic principle in all walks of life that structure and order facilitate good communication. Therefore, when you have the flow of inspiration in your essay, you must get this into a structure that will allow the marker to recognize the true quality of your work. For example, you might plan for an Introduction, Conclusion, three main headings and each of these with several sub-headings (see example below). Moreover, you may decide not to include your headings in your final presentation – i.e. just to use them initially to structure and balance your arguments. Once you have drafted this outline, you can then easily sketch an Introduction, and you will have been well prepared for the Conclusion when you arrive at that point.

> *A good structure will help you to balance the weight of each of your arguments against each other, and arrange your points in the order that will facilitate the fluent progression of your argument.*

Example – Write an essay that assesses the dynamics of globalization on the decision to outsource production

1. The quest to be on the top of corporate performance

   a. Outsourcing is a financial benefit.

   b. The uncertainty of world economies vs. gains from diversified business has to be considered.

   c. Returns are significant because of lower labour costs and higher diversity.

   d. There is an opportunity to streamline the company structure.

2. Compounded problems for first-time outsourcers

   a. There is a delay in financial gains through learning curve effects.

   b. There are social challenges in the home market concerning employment.

   c. Balancing cost reduction with quality standards has to be considered.

   d. The risks of international supply chain management are high compared to domestic.

3. The problem of competitive pressures

    a. Competitors are outsourcing.

    b. Competitors gain competitive advantage from cost and R&D opportunities.

    c. Herd behaviour and potential market access internationally have to be considered.

    d. There are conflicting reports in economic forecasts about risks and returns of outsourcing from competitors.

Finding major questions

When you are constructing a draft outline for an essay or project, you should consider the major question or questions you wish to address. It would be useful to make a list of all the issues that spring to mind that you might wish to tackle. The ability to design a good question is an art form that should be cultivated, and such questions will allow you to impress your assessor with the quality of your thinking.

If you construct your ideas around key questions, this will help you focus your mind and engage effectively with your subject. Your role will be like that of a detective, exploring the evidence and investigating the findings.

To illustrate the point, consider the example presented below. If you were asked to write an essay about the effectiveness of the police in your local community, you might as your starting point pose the following questions.

Example – The effectiveness of the police in the local community: initial questions

- Is there a high profile police presence?
- Are there regular 'on the beat' officers and patrol car activities?
- Do recent statistics show an increase or a decrease in crime in the area?
- Are the police involved in community activities and local schools?
- Does the local community welcome and support the police?

(Continued)

(Continued)

- Do the police have a good reputation for responding to calls?
- Do the police harass people unnecessarily?
- Do minority groups perceive the police to be fair?
- Do the police have an effective complaints procedure to deal with grievances against them?
- Do the police solicit and respond to local community concerns?

A similar line of thought leads you to enquire if companies internationalize successfully. It is your responsibility to transpose this type of thinking from commonplace to problem-specific questions in your classes.

Resting your case

It should be your aim to give the clear impression that your arguments are not based entirely on hunches, bias, feelings or intuition. In exams and essay questions, it is usually assumed (even if not directly specified) that you will appeal to evidence to support your claims. Therefore, when you write your essay, you should ensure that it is liberally sprinkled with citations and evidence. By the time the assessor reaches the end of your work, he or she should be convinced that your conclusions are evidence-based. A fatal flaw to be avoided is to make claims for which you have provided no authoritative source.

Give the clear impression that what you have asserted is derived from recognized sources (including up-to-date). It also looks impressive if you spread your citations across your essay rather than compressing them into a paragraph or two at the beginning and end.

Some examples of how you might introduce your evidence and sources are provided below:

- According to O'Neil (1999) ...
- Wilson (2003) has concluded that ...
- Taylor (2004) found that ...
- It has been claimed by McKibben (2002) that ...
- Appleby (2001) asserted that ...
- A review of the evidence by Lawlor (2004) suggests that ...
- Findings from a meta-analysis presented by Rea (2003) would indicate that .....

It is sensible to vary the expression used so that you are not monotonous and repetitive, and it also aids variety to introduce researchers' names at various places in the sentence (not always at the beginning). It is advisable to choose the expression that is most appropriate – for example, you can make a stronger statement about reviews that have identified recurrent and predominant trends in findings as opposed to one study that appears to run contrary to all the rest.

Credit is given for the use of caution and discretion where these are clearly needed.

Careful use of quotations

Although it is desirable to present a good range of cited sources, it is not judicious to present these as a 'patchwork quilt' – i.e. you just paste together what others have said with little thought for interpretative comment or coherent structure. It is a good general point to aim to avoid very lengthy quotes – short ones can be very effective. Aim at blending the quotations as naturally as possible into the flow of your sentences. Also it is good to vary your practices – sometimes use short, direct, brief quotes (cite the page number as well as the author and year), and at times you can summarize the gist of a quote in your own words. In this case, you should cite the author's name and year of publication but leave out quotation marks and the page number.

Use your quotes and evidence in a manner that demonstrates that you have thought the issues through, and have integrated them in a manner that shows you have been focused and selective in the use of your sources.

In terms of referencing, practice may vary from one discipline to the next, but some general points that will go a long way in contributing to good practice are:

- If a reference is cited in the text, it must be in the list at the end (and vice versa).
- Names and dates in the text should correspond exactly with the list in the References or Bibliography.
- The list of References or Bibliography should be in alphabetical order by the surname (not the initials) of the author or first author.
- Any reference you make in the text should be traceable by the reader (they should clearly be able to identify and trace the source).

A clearly defined Introduction

In an introduction to an essay, you have the opportunity to define the problem or issue that is being addressed and to set it within context. Resist the temptation to elaborate on any issue at the introductory stage. For example, think of a music composer who throws out hints and suggestions of the motifs that the orchestra will later develop. What he or she does in the Introduction is to provide little tasters of what will follow in order to whet the audience's appetite. If you go back to the analogy of the game of tennis, you can think of the Introduction as marking out the boundaries of the court in which the game is to be played.

> *If you leave the introduction and definition of your problem until the end of your writing, you will be better placed to map out the directions that will be taken.*

EXERCISE

An example for practice, if you wish, can be engaged if you look back at the drafted outline on assessing the dynamics of the housing market. Try to design an Introduction for that essay in about three or four sentences.

Conclusion – adding the finishing touches

In the conclusion, you should aim to tie your essay together in a clear and coherent manner. It is your last chance to leave an overall impression in your reader's mind. Therefore, you will at this stage want to do justice to your efforts and not sell yourself short. This is your opportunity to identify where the strongest evidence points or where the balance of probability lies. The conclusion to an exam question often has to be written hurriedly under the pressure of time, but with an essay (course work) you have time to reflect on, refine and adjust the content to your satisfaction. It should be your goal to make the conclusion a smooth finish that does justice to the range of content in summary and succinct form. Do not underestimate the value of an effective conclusion. 'Sign off' your essay in a manner that brings closure to the treatment of your subject.

> *The conclusion facilitates the chance to demonstrate where the findings have brought us to date, to highlight the issues that remain unresolved and to point to where future research should take us.*

Top-down and bottom-up clarity

An essay gives you the opportunity to refine each sentence and paragraph on your word processor. Each sentence is like a tributary that leads
into the stream of the paragraph that in turn leads into the mainstream
of the essay. From a 'top-down' perspective (i.e. starting at the top with
your major outline points), clarity is facilitated by the structure you draft
in your outline. You can ensure that the subheadings are appropriately
placed under the most relevant main heading, and that both sub- and
main headings are arranged in logical sequence. From a 'bottom-up' perspective (i.e. building up the details that 'flesh out' your main points),
you should check that each sentence is a 'feeder' for the predominant
concept in a given paragraph. When all this is done, you can check that
the transition from one point to the next is smooth rather than abrupt.

Checklist – Summary for essay writing

- ✓ Before you start – have a 'warm up' by tossing the issues around in your head.
- ✓ List the major concepts and link them in fluent form.
- ✓ Design a structure (outline) that will facilitate balance, progression, fluency and clarity.
- ✓ Pose questions and address these in critical fashion.
- ✓ Demonstrate that your arguments rest on evidence and spread cited sources across your essay.
- ✓ Provide an introduction that sets the scene and a conclusion that rounds off the arguments.

EXERCISE

Checklist – Attempt to write (or at least think about) some additional features
that would help facilitate good essay writing:

- ✓ ....
- ✓ ....
- ✓ ....
- ✓ ....
- ✓ ....

---

*In the above checklist, you could have features such as originality, clarity in
sentence and paragraph structure, applied aspects, addressing a subject you
feel passionately about and the ability to avoid going off on a tangent.*

| 3.4 | |
| revision hints and tips | |

This section will show you how to:

- map out your accumulated material for revision
- choose summary tags to guide your revision
- keep well-organized folders for revision
- make use of effective memory techniques
- prepare revision that combines bullet points and in-depth reading
- profit from the benefits of revising with others
- attend to the practical exam details that will help keep panic at bay
- use strategies that keep you task-focused during the exam
- select and apply relevant points from your prepared outlines.

The Return Journey

On a return journey, you will usually pass by all the same places that you had already passed when you were outward bound. If you had observed the various landmarks on your outward journey, you would be likely to remember them on your return. Similarly, revision is a means to 'revisit' what you have encountered before. Familiarity with your material can help reduce anxiety, inspire confidence and fuel motivation for further learning and good performance.

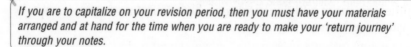

If you are to capitalize on your revision period, then you must have your materials arranged and at hand for the time when you are ready to make your 'return journey' through your notes.

Starting at the beginning

Your strategy for revision should be on your mind from your first lecture at the beginning of the academic semester. You should be like the squirrel that stores up nuts for the winter. Do not waste any lecture, tutorial, seminar, group discussion, etc. by letting the material evaporate into thin air. Get into the habit of making a few guidelines for revision after each learning activity. Keep a folder or file, or a little notebook that is reserved for revision and write out the major points that you have learned. By establishing this regular practice, you will find that what you have learned becomes consolidated in your mind, and you will also be in a better position to 'import' and 'export' your material both within and across subjects.

If you do this regularly, and do not make the task too tedious, you will be amazed at how much useful summary material you have accumulated when revision time comes.

Compiling summary notes

It would be useful and convenient to have a little notebook or cards on which you can write outline summaries that provide you with an overview of your subject at a glance. You could also use treasury tags to hold different batches of cards together while still allowing for inserts and re-sorting. Such practical resources can easily be slipped into your pocket or bag and produced when you are on the bus or train or while sitting in a traffic jam. They would also be useful if you are standing in a queue or waiting for someone who is not in a rush! A glance over your notes will consolidate your learning and will also activate your mind to think further about your subject. Therefore, it would also be useful to make a note of the questions that you would like to think about in greater depth. Your primary task is to get into the habit of constructing outline notes that will be useful for revision, and a worked example is provided on the next page.

There is a part of the mind that will continue to work on problems when you have moved on to focus on other issues. Therefore, if you feed on useful, targeted information, your mind will continue to work on 'automatic pilot' after you have 'switched off'.

Example – Part of a course on communication is the use of non-verbal communication, and your outline revision structure for this might be as follows

1. Aspects of non-verbal communication that run parallel with language:

   - pauses
   - tone of voice
   - inflection of voice
   - speed of voice.

2. Facets of non-verbal communication related to the use of body parts:

   - how close to stand to others
   - how much to use the hands
   - whether to make physical contact – e.g. touching, hugging, handshaking
   - the extent and frequency of eye contact.

3. General features that augment communication:

   - the use of smiles and frowns
   - the use of eyebrows
   - expressions of boredom or interest
   - dress and appearance.

Keeping organized records

People who have a fulfilled career have usually developed the twin skills of time and task management. It is worth pausing to remember that you can use your academic training to prepare for your future career in this respect. Therefore, ensure that you do not fall short of your potential because these qualities have not been cultivated. One important tactic is to keep a folder for each subject and divide this topic by topic. You can keep your topics in the same order in which they are presented in your course lectures. Bind them together in a ring binder or folder and use subject dividers to keep them apart. Make a numbered list of the contents at the beginning of the folder, and list each topic clearly as it marks a new section in your folder. Another important practice is to place all your notes on a given topic within the appropriate section – but don't put off this simple task; do it straightaway. Notes may come from lectures, seminars, tutorials, internet searches, personal notes, etc. It is also essential that when you remove these for consultation, you return them to their 'home' immediately after use.

> *Academic success has as much to do with good organization and planning, as it has to do with ability. The value of the quality material you have accumulated on your academic programme may be diminished because you have not organized it into an easily retrievable form.*

A fun example of an organized record – A history of romantic relationships

Factors may include:

- physical features my girlfriends/boyfriends have shared or differed in
- common and diverse personality characteristics
- shared and contrasting interests
- frequency of dates with each
- places frequented together
- contact with both circles of friends
- use of humour in our communication
- frequency and resolution of conflicts
- mutual generosity
- courtesy and consideration
- punctuality
- dress and appearance.

Let's imagine that you had five girlfriends or boyfriends over the last few years. Each of the five names could be included under all of the above subjects. You could then compare them with each other, looking at what they had in common and how they differed. Moreover, you could think of the ones you liked best and least, and then look through your dossier to establish why this might have been. You could also judge who had most and least in common with you and whether you are more attracted to those who differed most from you. The questions open to you can go on and on. The real point here is that you will have gathered a wide variety of material that is organized in such a way that will allow you to use a range of evidence to come up with some satisfactory and authoritative conclusions – if that is possible in matters so directly related to the heart!

Using past papers

Revision will be very limited if it is confined to memory work. You should by all means read over your revision cards or notebook and keep the picture of the major facts in front of your mind's eye. It is also, however, essential that you become familiar with previous exam papers so that you will have some idea of how the questions are likely to be framed. Therefore, build up a good range of past exam papers (especially recent ones) and add these to your folder. When cows and sheep have grazed, they lie down and 'chew the cud'. That is, they regurgitate what they have eaten and take time to digest the food thoroughly.

> *If you think over previous exam questions, this will help you not only recall what you have deposited in your memory, but also to develop your understanding of the issues. The questions from past exam papers, and further questions that you have developed yourself, will allow you to 'chew the cud'.*

Worked example – Evaluate the pleasures and problems of keeping a pet

Immediately, you can see that you will require two lists and you can begin to work on documenting your reasons under each as below:

Problems

- vet and food bills
- restrictions on holidays/weekends away
- friends may not visit
- allergies
- smells and cleanliness
- worries about leaving pet alone.

Pleasures

- companionship
- fun and relaxation
- satisfaction from caring
- cuddles
- contact with other pet owners
- good distraction from problems.

You will also have noticed that the word 'evaluate' is in the question, so your mind must go to work on making judgements. You may decide to work through problems first and then through pleasures, or it may be your preference to compare point by point as you go along. Whatever conclusion you come to may be down to personal subjective preference but at least you will have worked through all the issues from both standpoints. The lesson is to ensure that part of your revision should include critical thinking as well as memory work. Our example of outsourcing above can easily be used to train this: try out your critical thinking skills in a discussion about the economic and social benefits and challenges that outsourcing holds. Use your notes from the example of outsourcing above, but also think further.

> *You cannot think adequately without the raw materials provided by your memory deposits.*

Employing effective mnemonics (memory aids)

The Greek word from which 'mnemonics' is derived refers to a tomb – a structure that is built in memory of a loved one, friend or respected person. 'Mnemonics' can be simply defined as aids to memory – devices that will help you recall information that might otherwise be difficult to retrieve from memory. For example, if you find an old toy in the attic of your house, it may suddenly trigger a flood of childhood memories associated with it. Mnemonics can therefore be thought of as keys that open the memory's storehouse.

Visualization is one technique that can be used to aid memory. For example, the Location Method is where a familiar journey is visualized and you can 'place' the facts that you wish to remember at various landmarks along the journey – e.g. a bus stop, a car park, a shop, a store, a bend, a police station, a traffic light, etc. This has the advantage of making an association of the information you have to learn with other material that is already firmly embedded and structured in your memory. Therefore, once the relevant memory is activated, a dynamic 'domino effect' will be triggered. However, there is no reason why you cannot use a whole toolkit of mnemonics. Some examples and illustrations of these are presented below.

1. If you can arrange your subject matter in a logical sequence, this will ensure that your series of facts will also connect with each other and one will trigger the other in recall. 2. You can use memory devices either at the stage of initial learning or when you later return to consolidate.

Location Method – defined above.

Visualization – turning information into pictures, e.g. the example given about the problems and pleasures of pets could be envisaged as two tug-of-war teams that pull against each other. You could visualize each player as an argument and have the label written on his or her tee shirt. The war could start with two players and then be joined by another two and so on. In addition, you could compare each player's weight to the strength of each argument. You might also want to make use of colour – use your favourite colour for the winning team and the colour you dislike most for the losers!

Alliteration's artful aid – finding a series of words that all begin with the same letter. See the example below related to the experiments of Ebbinghaus.

Peg system – 'hanging' information onto a term so that when you hear the term, you will remember the ideas connected with it (an umbrella term). In the example on ageing, there were four different types: biological, chronological, sociological and psychological. Under biological, you could remember menopause, hair loss, wrinkling, vision loss, hearing deterioration, etc.

Hierarchical system – this is a development of the previous point with higher order, middle order and lower order terms. For example, you could think of the continents of the world (higher order), and then group these into the countries under them (middle order). Under countries, you could have cities, rivers and mountains (lower order).

Acronyms – taking the first letter of all the key words and making a word from these. An example from business is SWOT: Strengths, Weaknesses, Opportunities and Threats.

Mind maps – these have become very popular and allow you to draw lines that stretch out from the central idea and to develop the subsidiary ideas in the same way. It is a little like the pegging and hierarchical methods combined and turned sideways! The method has the advantage of giving you the complete picture at a glance, although it can become a complex work of art!

Rhymes and chimes – words that rhyme and words that end with a similar sound (e.g. commemoration, celebration, anticipation). These provide another dimension to memory work by including sound. Memory can be enhanced when information is processed in various modalities – e.g. hearing, seeing, speaking, visualizing.

A confidence booster

At the end of the 19th century, Ebbinghaus and his assistant memorized lists of nonsense words (which could not be remembered by being attached to meaning), and then endeavoured to recall these. What they discovered was that:

- some words could be recalled freely from memory while others appeared to be forgotten
- words that could not be recalled were later recognized as belonging to the lists (i.e. were not new additions)
- when the lists were jumbled into a different sequence, the experimenters were able to re-jumble them into the original sequence
- when the words that were 'forgotten' were learned again, the learning process was much easier the second time round (i.e. there was evidence of re-learning savings).

The four points of this experiment can be remembered by alliteration: Recall, Recognition, Reconstruction and Re-learning savings. This experiment has been described as a confidence booster because it demonstrates that memory is more powerful than is often imagined, especially when we consider that Ebbinghaus and his assistant did not have the advantage of processing the meaning of the words.

Alternating between methods

It is not sufficient to present outline points in response to an exam question (although it is better to do this as nothing if you have run out of time in your exam). Your aim should be to put 'meat on the bones' by adding substance, evidence and arguments to your basic points. You should work at finding a balance between the two methods – outline revision cards might be best reserved for short bus journeys, whereas extended reading might be better employed for longer revision slots at home or in the library. Your ultimate goal should be to bring together an effective, working approach that will enable you to face your exam questions comprehensively and confidently.

> *In revision, it is useful to alternate between scanning over your outline points, and reading through your notes, articles, chapters, etc in an in-depth manner. Also, the use of different times, places and methods will provide you with the variety that might prevent monotony and facilitate freshness.*

Worked example – Imagine that you are doing a course on the human body

Your major outline topics might be:

- the names, position and purpose of bones in the body
- the names and position of organs in the body
- the organs and chemicals associated with digestion
- composition, function and routes of blood
- parts and processes of the body associated with breathing
- components and dynamics of the nervous and lymphatic systems
- the structure, nature and purpose of the skin
- the role of the brain in controlling and mediating the above systems.

This outline would be your overall, bird's-eye view of the course. You could then choose one of the topics and have all your key terms under that. For example, under digestion, you might have listed: mouth, oesophagus, stomach, duodenum, intestine, liver, vagus nerve, hypothalamus, hydrochloric acid and carbohydrates. In order to move from memory to understanding, you would need to consider the journey of food through the human digestive system. In the same manner, international market research can be organized, and an outline would allow you to move from memory to understanding if you consider the value chain of the company as well as its market segmentation and consumers throughout its locations, determining motivations for localization in one market rather than another.

If you alternate between memory work and reading, you will soon be able to think through the processes by just looking at your outlines.

Revising with others

If you can find a few other students to revise with, this will provide another fresh approach to the last stages of your learning. First ensure that others carry their workload and are not merely using the hard work of others as a shortcut to success. Of course, you should think of group sessions as one of the strings on your violin, but not the only string. This collective approach would allow you to assess your strengths and weaknesses (showing you where you are off track), and to benefit from the resources and insights of others. Before you meet up, you can each design some questions for the whole group to address. The group could also go through past exam papers and discuss the points that might provide an effective response to each question. It should not be the aim of the group to provide standard and identical answers for each group member to mimic. Group work is currently deemed to be advantageous by educationalists, and teamwork is held to be a desirable quality by employers.

Each individual should aim to use their own style and content while drawing on and benefiting from the group's resources.

EXERCISE

Make a list of the advantages and disadvantages of revising in small groups.

Advantages	Disadvantages
1.	1. ....
2.	2. ....
3.	3. ....
4.	4. ....
5.	5. ....

Can the disadvantages be eliminated or at least minimized?

Checklist – Good study habits for revision time

✓ Set a date for the 'official' beginning of revision and prepare for 'revision mode'.

✓ Do not force cramming by leaving revision too late.

✓ Take breaks from revision to avoid saturation.

✓ Indulge in relaxing activities to give your mind a break from pressure.

✓ Minimize or eliminate the consumption of alcohol during the revision season.

✓ Get into a good rhythm of sleep to allow renewal of your mind.

✓ Avoid excessive caffeine especially at night so that sleep is not disrupted.

✓ Try to adhere to regular eating patterns.

✓ Try to have a brisk walk in fresh air each day (e.g. in the park).

✓ Avoid excessive dependence on junk food and snacks.

EXERCISE

Write your own checklist of what you can add to the revision process to ensure it is not just a memory exercise.

✓ ....

✓ ....

✓ ....

✓ ....

✓ ....

In the above exercise, what you could add to memory work during revision might include using past exam papers, setting problem-solving tasks, doing drawings to show connections and directions between various concepts, explaining concepts to student friends in joint revision sessions, and devising your own mock exam questions.

3.5	
exam tips	

This section will show you how to:

- develop strategies for controlling your nervous energy
- tackle worked examples of time and task management in exams
- attend to the practical details associated with the exam
- stay focused on the exam questions
- link revision outlines to strategy for addressing exam questions.

Handling your nerves

Exam nerves are not unusual and it has been concluded that test anxiety arises because of the perception that your performance is being evaluated, that the consequences are likely to be serious and that you are working under the pressure of a time restriction. However, it has also been asserted that the activation of the autonomic nervous system is adaptive in that is designed to prompt us to take action in order to avoid danger. If you focus on the task at hand, rather than on feeding a downward negative spiral in your thinking patterns, this will help you keep your nerves under control. In the run up to your exams, you can practice some simple relaxation techniques that will help you bring stress under control.

It is a very good thing if you can interpret your nervous reactions positively, as the symptoms are more likely to be problematic if you interpret them negatively, pay too much attention to them or allow them to interfere with your exam preparation or performance.

Some practices that may help reduce or buffer the effects of exam stress are:

- listening to music
- going for a brisk walk or taking some exercise

- simple breathing exercises
- some muscle relaxation
- watching a movie
- laughing
- relaxing in a bath (with music if preferred).

The best choice is going to be the one (or the combination) that works best for you – perhaps to be discovered by trial and error. Some of the above techniques can be practised on the morning of the exam, and even the memory of them can be used just before the exam. For example, you could run over a relaxing tune in your head, and have this echo inside you as you enter the exam room. The idea behind all this is that, first, stress levels must come down, and second, relaxing thoughts will serve to displace stressful reactions. It has been said that stress is the body's call to take action, but anxiety is a maladaptive response to that call.

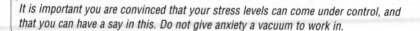

It is important you are convinced that your stress levels can come under control, and that you can have a say in this. Do not give anxiety a vacuum to work in.

Time management with examples

The all-important matter as you approach an exam is to develop the belief that you can take control of the situation. As you work through the list of issues that you need to address, you will be able to tick them off one by one. One of the issues you will need to be clear about before the exam is the length of time you should allocate to each question. Sometimes this can be quite simple (although it is always necessary to read the rubric carefully) – e.g. if two questions are to be answered in a two-hour paper, you should allow one hour for each question. If it is a two-hour paper with one essay question and 5 shorter answers, you could allow one hour for the essay and 12 minutes each for the shorter questions. However, you always need to check out the weighting for the marks on each question, and you will also need to deduct whatever time it takes you to read over the paper and to choose your questions. See if you can work out a time management strategy in each of the following scenarios. More importantly, give yourself some practice on the papers you are likely to face.

Remember to check if the structure of your exam paper is the same as in previous years, and do not forget that excessive time in your 'strongest' question may not compensate for very poor answers to other questions. Also ensure that you read the rubric carefully in the exam.

EXERCISE

Examples for working out the division of exam labour by time.

1. A three-hour paper with four compulsory questions (equally weighted in marks)
2. A three-hour paper with two essays and 10 short questions (each of the three sections carry one third of the marks)
3. A two-hour paper with two essay questions and 100 multiple-choice questions (half the marks are on the two essays and half the marks are on the multiple-choice section)

Get into the calculating frame of mind and be sure to have the calculations done before the exam. Ensure that the structure of the exam has not changed since the last one. Also, deduct the time taken to read over the paper in allocating time to each question.

Suggested answers to previous exercise:

1 This allows 45 minutes for each question (4 questions × 45 minutes = 3 hours). However, if you allow 40 minutes for each question this will give you 20 minutes (4 questions × 5 minutes) to read over the paper and plan your outlines.

2 In this example, you can spend 1 hour on each of the two major questions, and 1 hour on the 10 short questions. For the two major questions, you could allow 10 minutes for reading and planning on each, and 50 minutes for writing. In the 10 short questions, you could allow 6 minutes in total for each (10 questions × 6 minutes = 60 minutes). However, if you allow approximately 1 minute reading and planning time, this will allow 5 minutes' writing time for each question.

3 In this case, you have to divide 120 minutes by 3 questions – this allows 40 minutes for each. You could, for example, allow 5 minutes' reading/planning time for each essay and 35 minutes for writing (or 10 minutes reading/planning and 30 minutes writing). After you have completed the two major questions, you are left with 40 minutes to tackle the 100 multiple-choice questions.

You may not be able to achieve total precision in planning time for tasks, but you will have a greater feeling of control and confidence if you have some reference points to guide you.

Task management with examples

After you have decided on the questions you wish to address, you then need to plan your answers. Some students prefer to plan all outlines and draft work at the beginning, while others prefer to plan and address one answer before proceeding to address the next question. Decide on your strategy before you enter the exam room and stick to your plan. When you have done your draft outline as rough work, you should allocate an appropriate time for each section. This will prevent you from excessive treatment of some aspects while falling short on other parts. Such careful planning will help you achieve balance, fluency and symmetry.

Keep an awareness of time limitations and this will help you to write succinctly, keep focused on the task and prevent you dressing up your responses with unnecessary padding.

Some students put as much effort into their rough work as they do into their exam essay.

An overelaborate mind map may give the impression that the essay is little more than a repetition of this detailed structure, and that the quality of the content has suffered because too much time was spent on the plan.

Example – Try the following exercise

Work out the time allocation for the following outline, allowing for one hour on the question. Deduct 10 minutes taken at the beginning for choice and planning.

Discuss whether it is justifiable to ban cigarette smoking in pubs and restaurants.

1. Arguments for a ban

    a. Health risks by sustained exposure to passive smoking.
    b. Employees (such as students) suffer unfairly.
    c. Children accompanied by adults may also be victims.

2. Arguments against a ban

    a. Risks may be exaggerated.
    b. Dangerous chemicals and pollutants in the environment are ignored by governments.
    c. Non-smokers can choose whether to frequent smoking venues.

3. Qualifying suggestions

    a. There could be better use of ventilation and extractor fans.
    b. There could be designated non-smoking areas.
    c. Pubs and restaurants should be addressed separately in relation to a ban.

Attending to practical details

This short section is designed to remind you of the practical details that should be attended to in preparation for an exam. There are always students who turn up late, or to the wrong venue or for the wrong exam, or do not turn up at all! Check and re-check that you have all the details of each exam correctly noted. What you don't need is to arrive late and then have to tame your panic reactions. The exam season is the time when you should aim to be at your best.

Turn up to the right venue in good time so that you can quieten your mind and bring your stress levels under control.

Make note of the following details and check that you have taken control of each one.

Checklist – Practical exam details

✓ Check that you have the correct venue.

✓ Make sure you know how to locate the venue before the exam day.

✓ Ensure that the exam time you have noted is accurate.

✓ Allow sufficient time for your journey and consider the possibility of delays.

✓ Bring an adequate supply of stationery and include back up.

✓ Bring a watch for your time and task management.

✓ Bring some liquid such as a small bottle of still water, if required.

✓ Bring some tissues, if required.

✓ Observe whatever exam regulations your university/college has set in place.

✓ Fill in required personal details before the exam begins.

Controlling wandering thoughts

In a simple study conducted in the 1960s, Ganzer (1968) found that students who frequently lifted their heads and looked away from their scripts during exams tended to perform poorly. This makes sense because it implies that the students were taking too much time out when they should have been on task. One way to fail your exam is to get up and walk out of the test room, but another way is to 'leave' the test room mentally by being preoccupied with distracting thoughts. The distracting thoughts may be either related to the exam itself or totally irrelevant to it. The net effect of both these forms of intrusion is to distract you from the task at hand and debilitate your test performance. Read over the two lists of distracting thoughts presented below.

Typical Test-relevant Thoughts (Evaluative)

- I wish I had prepared better.
- What will the examiner think?
- Others are doing better than me.
- What I am writing is nonsense.
- I can't remember important details.

Characteristic Test-irrelevant Thoughts (Non-evaluative)

- I am looking forward to this weekend.
- Which DVD should I watch tonight?
- His remark really annoyed me yesterday.
- I wonder how the game will go on Saturday.
- I wonder if he/she really likes me.

Research has consistently shown that distracting, intrusive thoughts during an exam are more detrimental to performance than stressful symptoms such as sweaty palms, dry mouth, tension, trembling, etc. Moreover, it does not matter whether the distracting thoughts are negative evaluations related to the exam or are totally irrelevant to the exam. The latter may be a form of escape from the stressful situation.

Practical suggestions for controlling wandering thoughts

- Be aware that this problem is detrimental to performance.
- Do not look around to find distractions.
- If distracted, write down 'keep focused on the task'.
- If distracted again, look back at the above and continue to do this.
- Start to draft rough work as soon as you can.
- If you struggle with initial focus, then re-read or elaborate on your rough work.
- If you have commenced your essay, re-read the last paragraph (or two) that you've written.
- Do not throw fuel on your distracting thoughts – starve them by re-engaging with the task at hand.

Links to revision

If you have followed the guidelines given for revision, you will be well equipped with outline plans when you enter the exam room. You may have chosen to use headings and subheadings, mind maps, hierarchical approaches or just a series of simple mnemonics. Whatever method you choose to use, you should be furnished with a series of memory triggers that will open the treasure house door for you once you begin to write.

> Although you may have clear templates with a definite structure or framework for organizing your material, you will need to be flexible about how this should be applied to your exam questions.

For example, imagine that films are one of the topics that you will be examined on. You decide to memorize lists of films that you are familiar with under categorical headings in the following manner.

Romantic comedy	War/History/Fantasy	Space/Alien invasion
Notting Hill	Braveheart	Star Wars
Pretty Woman	Gladiator	Independence Day
Along Came Polly	First Knight	Alien
Four Weddings and a Funeral	Troy	Men in Black

Adventure/Fantasy	Horror/Supernatural
Harry Potter	Poltergeist
Lord of the Rings	The Omen
Alice in Wonderland	Sixth Sense
Labyrinth	What Lies Beneath

The basic mental template might be these and a few other categories. You know that you will not need every last detail, although you may need to select a few from each category. For example, you might be asked to:

a. compare and contrast features of comedy and horror
b. comment on films that have realistic moral lessons in them
c. identify films that might be construed as a propaganda exercise
d. identify films where the characters are more important than the plot and vice versa.

Some questions will put a restriction on the range of categories you can use (a), while others will allow you to dip into any category (b, c and d). A question about fantasy would allow you scope across various categories.

If we transpose this example to IB, you might apply the above technique to memorize the various entry modes that companies use in internationalization. Questions such as those designed for you to analyse the market-seeking behaviour of corporations will here allow you scope across various categories.

> *Restrict your material to what is relevant to the question, but bear in mind that this may allow you some scope.*

The art of 'name dropping'

In most topics at business school/university, you will be required to cite studies as evidence for your arguments and to link these to the names of researchers, scholars or theorists. It will help if you can use the correct dates or at least the decades, and it is good to demonstrate that you have used contemporary sources, and have done some independent work. A marker will have dozens if not hundreds of scripts to work through and they will know if you are just repeating the same phrases from the same sources as everyone else. There is inevitably a certain amount of this that must go on, but there is room for you to add fresh and original touches that demonstrate independence and imagination.

Give the clear impression that you have done more than the bare minimum and that you have enthusiasm for the subject. Also, spread the use of researchers' names across your exam essay rather than compressing them into, for example, the first and last paragraphs.

Flight, fight or freeze

As previously noted, the autonomic nervous system (ANS) is activated when danger or apparent danger is imminent. Of course, the threat does not have to be physical, as in the case of an exam, a job interview, a driving test or a TV appearance. Indeed, the ANS can be activated even at the anticipation of a future threat. However, the reaction is more likely to be stronger as you enter into the crucial time of testing or challenge. Symptoms may include deep breathing, trembling, headaches, nausea, tension, dry mouth and palpitations. How should we react to these once they have been triggered? A postman might decide to run away from a barking dog and run the risk of being chased and bitten. A second possible response is to freeze on the spot – this might arrest the animal in its tracks, but is no use in an exam situation. In contrast, to fight might not be the best strategy against the dog, but will be more productive in an exam. That is, you are going into the exam room to 'tackle' the questions, and not to run away from the challenge before you.

The final illustration below uses the analogy of archery to demonstrate how you might take control in an exam.

Lessons from Archery

- Enter the exam room with a quiver full of arrows – this is all the points you will need to use.
- Eye up the target board you are to shoot at – choose the exam questions.
- Stand in a good position for balance and vision – prepare your time management.
- Prepare your bow and arrow and take aim at the target – keep focused on the task at hand and do not be sidetracked.
- Pull the string of the bow back to get maximum thrust on the arrow – match your points to the appropriate question.
- Aim to hit the board where the best marks are (bull's eye or close) – do not be content with the minimum standard such as a mere pass.
- Pull out arrows and shoot one after another to gain maximum hits and advantage – do not be content with preparing one or two strong points.
- Make sure your arrows are sharp and the supporting bow and string are firm – choose relevant points and support with evidence.
- Avoid wasted effort by loose and careless shots – do not dress up your essay with unnecessary padding.

EXERCISE

Write your own checklist on the range of combined skills and personal qualities that you will need to be at your best in an exam.

✓ ....

✓ ....

✓ ....

✓ ....

✓ ....

With reference to the above exercise, skills might include such things as critical thinking, time and task management, focus on issues, and quick identification of problems to address. Personal qualities might include factors such as confidence, endurance, resilience and stress control.

3.6

tips on interpreting essay and exam questions

This section will show you how to:

- focus on the issues that are relevant and central
- read questions carefully and take account of all the words
- produce a balanced critique in your outline structures
- screen for the key words that will shape your response
- focus on different shades of meaning between 'critique', 'evaluate', 'discuss' and 'compare and contrast'.

What do you see?

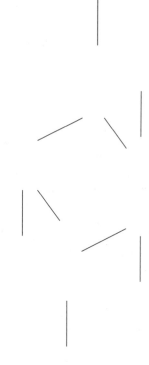

The suggested explanation for visual illusions is the inappropriate use of cues – i.e. we try to interpret three-dimensional figures in the real world with the limitations of a two-dimensional screen (the retina in the eye). We use cues such as shade, texture, size, background, etc. to interpret distance, motion, shape, etc., and we sometimes use these inappropriately. Another visual practice we engage in is to 'fill in the blanks' or join up the lines (as in the case of the image of the nine lines above, we might assume it to be a chair). Our tendency is to impose the nearest similar and familiar template on that which we think we see. The same occurs in the social world – when we are introduced to someone of a different race, we may (wrongly) assume certain things about them. The same can also apply to the way you read exam or essay questions. In these cases, you are required to 'fill in the blanks' but what you fill in may be the wrong interpretation of the question. This is especially likely if you have primed yourself to expect certain questions to appear in an exam, but it can also happen in course work essays. Although examiners do not deliberately design questions to trick you or trip you up, they cannot always prevent you from seeing things that were not designed to be there. When one student was asked what the four seasons are, the response given was, 'salt, pepper, mustard and vinegar'. This was not quite what the examiner had in mind!

> Go into the exam room, or address the course work essay, well prepared, but be flexible enough to structure your learned material around the slant of the question.

A politician's answer

Politicians are renowned for refusing to answer questions directly or for evading them through raising other questions. A humorous example is given of when a politician was asked, 'is it true that you always answer questions by asking another?', the reply was, 'who told you that?' Therefore, make sure that you answer the set question, although there may be other questions that arise out of this for further study that you might want to highlight in your conclusion. As a first principle, you must answer the set question and not another question that you had hoped for in the exam or essay.

> Do not leave the examiner feeling like the person who interviews a politician and goes away with the impression that the important issues have been sidestepped.

Example – Discuss strategies for improving the sale of fresh fruit and vegetables in the market place at the point of delivery to the customer

Directly relevant points

- the stall and produce being kept clean
- well presented/arranged produce
- the use of colour and variety
- the position of the stall in the market (e.g. smells)
- the use of free samples
- the appearance and manner of assistants
- competitive prices.

Less relevant points

- the advantages of organic growth
- arguments for vegetarianism
- cheaper transport for produce
- the value of locally grown produce
- strategies for pest control in growth
- arguments for refrigeration in transit
- cheaper rents for markets.

Although some of the points listed in the second column may be relevant to sales overall, they are not as directly relevant to sales 'in the market place at the point of delivery to the customer'. If the question had included the quality of the produce, then some of those issues should be addressed. Also, it could be argued that some of these issues could be highlighted on a board at the stall, e.g. 'Only organically grown produce is sold at this stall'. So some of the points could be mentioned briefly in this way without going off on a tangent.

Be ready to resist the wealth of fascinating material at your disposal that is not directly relevant to your question.

Missing your question

A student bitterly complained after an exam that the topic he had revised so thoroughly had not been tested in the exam. The first response to that is that students should always cover enough topics to avoid selling themselves short in the exam – the habit of 'question spotting' is always a risky game to play. However, the reality in the anecdotal example was that the question the student was looking for was there, but he had not seen it. He had expected the question to be couched in certain terms and he could not find these when he scanned over the questions in blind panic. Therefore, the simple lesson is to always read over the questions carefully, slowly and thoughtfully. This practice is time well spent.

> *You can miss the question if you restrict yourself to looking for a set form of words and if you do not read over all the words carefully.*

Writing it down

If you write down the question you have chosen to address, and perhaps quietly articulate it with your lips, you are more likely to process fully its true meaning and intent. Think of how easy it is to misunderstand a question that had been put to you verbally because you have misinterpreted the tone or emphasis.

> *If you read over the question several times, you should be aware of all the key words and will begin to sense the connections between the ideas, and will envisage the possible directions you could take in your response.*

Take the following humorous example:

a. What is that on the road ahead?
b. What is that on the road, a head?

Question (a) calls for the identification of an object (what is that?), but question (b) has converted this into an object that suggests there has been a decapitation! Ensure therefore that you understand the direction the question is pointing you in so that you do not go off at a tangent. One word in the question that is not properly attended to can throw you completely off track as in the following example:

a. Discuss whether the love of money is the root of all evil.

b. Discuss whether money is the root of all evil.

These are two completely different questions, as (a) suggests that the real problem with money is inherent in faulty human use – that is, money itself may not be a bad thing if it is used as a servant and not a master, whereas (b) may suggest that behind every evil act that has ever been committed, money is likely to have been implicated somewhere in the motive.

Pursuing a critical approach

In degree courses, you are usually expected to write critically rather than merely descriptively, although it may be necessary to use some minimal descriptive substance as the raw material for your debate.

Example – Evaluate the evidence as to whether the American astronauts really walked on the moon, or whether this was a stage-managed hoax in a studio

Arguments for studio

- Was a flag really blowing on the moon?
- Explain the shadows.
- Why were no stars seen?
- Why was there little dust blowing on landing?
- Can humans survive passing through the radiation belt?

Arguments for walking

- Communications with laser reflectors were left on the moon.
- The retrieved rocks show patterns that are not earthly.
- How could such a hoax be protected?
- The American activities were monitored by the Soviets.
- There are plausible explanations for the arguments against walking.

Given that the question is about a critical evaluation of the evidence, you would need to address the issues one by one from both standpoints. What you should not do is digress into a tangent about the physical characteristics of the Beagle spaceship or the astronauts' suits. Neither should you be drawn into a lengthy description of lunar features and contours even if you have in-depth knowledge of these.

Analysing the parts

In an effective sports team, the end product is always greater than the sum of the parts. Similarly, a good essay cannot be constructed without reference to the parts. Furthermore, the parts will arise as you break down the question into the components it suggests to you. Although the breaking down of a question into components is not sufficient for an excellent essay, it is a necessary starting point.

> *To achieve a good response to an exam or essay question, aim to integrate all the individual issues presented in a manner that gives shape and direction to your efforts.*

Example 1 – Discuss whether the creation and preservation of tax-free zones is justified

Two parts to this question are clearly suggested – creation and preservation, and you would need to do justice to each in your answer. Other issues that arise in relation to these are left for you to suggest and discuss. Examples might be finance, prioritization, emerging market issues, local and international infrastrucutures, and logistics.

Example 2 – Evaluate the advantages and disadvantages of giving students course credit for participation in experiments

This is a straightforward question in that you have two major sections – advantages and disadvantages. You are left with the choice of the issues that you wish to address, and you can arrange these in the order you prefer. Your aim should be to ensure that you do not have a lopsided view of this, even if you feel quite strongly one way or the other.

Example 3 – Trace in a critical manner western society's changing attitudes to the corporal punishment of children

In this case, you might want to consider the role of governments, the church, schools, parents and the media. However, you will need to have some reference points to the past as you are asked to address the issue of change. There would also be scope to look at where the strongest influences for change arise and where the strongest resistance comes from. You might argue that the changes have been dramatic or evolutionary.

Give yourself plenty of practice at thinking of questions in this kind of way – both with topics on and not on your course. Topics not on your course that really interest you may be a helpful way to 'break you in' to this critical way of thinking.

Luchins and learning sets

In a series of experiments, Luchins allowed children to learn how to solve a problem that involved pouring water from and into a series of jugs of various sizes and shapes. He then gave them other problems that could be solved by following the same sequence. However, when he later gave them another problem that could be solved through a simpler sequence, they went about solving it through the previously learned procedure. In this case, the original approach was more difficult but it had become so set in the children's minds that they were blinded to the shorter, more direct route.

Example – How much did the wealthy Scottish man leave behind?

The story is told of a wealthy Scottish man who died, and no one in his village knew how much he had left behind. The issue was debated and gossiped about for some time, but one man claimed that he knew how much the man had left. He teased all the debaters and gossips in the village night after night. Eventually, he let his big secret out, and the answer was that the rich man had left 'all of it' behind! No one in the village had been able to work out the mischievous man's little ruse because of the convergent thinking style they used. Some exam questions may require you to be divergent in the way you think (i.e. there is not just one obvious solution to the problem). This may mean being like a detective in the way you investigate and problem solve. The only difference is that you may need to set up the problem as well as the solution!

> *Get into the habit of 'stepping sideways' and looking at questions from several angles. The best way to do this is by practice, e.g. on previous exam papers.*

Checklist – Ensuring that questions are understood before being fully addressed

✓ Read over the chosen question several times.

✓ Write it down to ensure that it is clear.

✓ Check that you have not omitted any important aspect or point of emphasis.

✓ Ensure that you do not wrongly impose preconceived expectations on the question.

✓ Break the question into parts (dismantle and rebuild).

EXERCISE

Write your own checklist on any additional points of guidance for exams that you have picked up from tutors or textbooks.

✓ ....

✓ ....

✓ ....

✓ ....

✓ ....

When asked to discuss

Students often ask how much of their own opinion they should include in an essay. In a discussion, when you raise one issue, another one can arise out of it. One tutor used to introduce his lectures by saying that he was going to 'unpack' the arguments. When you unpack an object (such as a new desk that has to be assembled), you first remove the overall packaging, such as a large box, and then proceed to remove the covers from all the component parts. After that, you attempt to assemble all the parts, according to the given design, so that they hold together in the intended manner. In a discussion, your aim should be not just to identify and define all the parts that contribute, but also to show where they fit (or don't fit) into the overall picture.

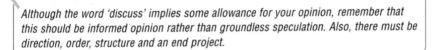

Although the word 'discuss' implies some allowance for your opinion, remember that this should be informed opinion rather than groundless speculation. Also, there must be direction, order, structure and an end project.

Checklist – Features of a response to a 'discuss' question

✓ contains a chain of issues that lead into each other in sequence

✓ has clear shape and direction which unfold in the progression of the argument

✓ is underpinned by reference to findings and certainties

✓ contains an identification of issues where doubt remains

✓ has a tone of argument which may be tentative but should not be vague.

If a critique is requested

One example that might help clarify what is involved in a critique is the hotly debated topic of the physical punishment of children. It would be important in the interest of balance and fairness to present all sides and shades of the argument. You would then look at whether there is available evidence to support each argument, and you might introduce issues that have been coloured by prejudice, tradition, religion and legislation. It would be an aim to identify emotional arguments, arguments based on intuition and to get down to those arguments that really have solid evidence-based support. Finally, you would want to flag up where the strongest evidence appears to lie, and you should also identify issues that appear to be inconclusive. It would be expected that you should, if possible, arrive at some certainties.

Write your own summary checklist for the features of a critique. You can either summarize the above points, or use your own points or a mixture of the two.

✓ ....

✓ ....

✓ ....

✓ ....

✓ ....

If asked to compare and contrast

When asked to compare and contrast, you should be thinking in terms of similarities and differences. You should ask what the two issues share in common, and what features of each are distinct. Your preferred strategy for tackling this might be to work first through all the similarities and then through all the contrasts (or vice versa). Alternatively, you could work through a similarity and a contrast, followed by another similarity and contrast, etc.

Example – Compare and contrast the uses of tea and coffee as beverages

Similarities

- They are usually drunk hot.
- They can be drunk without food.
- They can be taken with a snack or meal.
- They can be drunk with milk.
- They can be taken with honey, sugar or sweeteners.
- They both contain caffeine.
- They can both be addictive.

Contrasts

- There are differences in taste.
- Tea is perhaps preferred at night.

- There are differences in caffeine content.
- Coffee is more bitter.
- Coffee is sometimes taken with cream or whisky.
- Each is perhaps preferred with different foods.
- Coffee is preferred for a hangover.

When you compare and contrast, you should aim to paint a true picture of the full 'landscape'.

Whenever evaluation is requested

A worked example of evaluation – TV soap opera director

Imagine that you are a TV director for a popular soap opera. You have observed in recent months that you have lost some viewers to an alternative soap opera on a rival channel. All is not yet lost because you still have a loyal hardcore of viewers who have remained faithful. Your programme has been broadcast for 10 years and there has, until recently, been little change in viewing figures. The rival programme has used some fresh ideas and new actors and has a big novelty appeal. It will take time to see if their level of viewing can be sustained, but you run the risk that you might lose some more viewers at least in the short term. On the other hand, with some imagination, you might be able to attract some viewers back. However, there have been some recent murmurings about aspects of the programme being stale, repetitive and predictable. You have been given the task of evaluating the programme to see if you can ascertain why you have retained the faithful but lost other viewers, and what you could do to improve the programme without compromising the aspects that work. In your task, you might want to review past features (retrospective), outline present features (perspective) and envisage positive future changes (prospective). This illustration may provoke you to think about how you might

(Continued)

(Continued)

approach a question that asks you to evaluate some theory or concept in your own academic field of study. Some summary points to guide you are presented below:

- Has the theory/concept stood the test of time?
- Is there a supportive evidence base that would not easily be overturned?
- Are there questionable elements that have been or should be challenged?
- Does more recent evidence point to a need for modification?
- Is the theory/concept robust and likely to be around for the foreseeable future?
- Could it be strengthened through being merged with other theories/concepts?

EXERCISE

Write your own checklist on what you remember or understand about each of the following: 'discuss', 'compare and contrast', 'evaluate' and 'critique' (just a key word or two for each). If you find this difficult, then you should read the section again and then try the exercise.

✓ ....

✓ ....

✓ ....

✓ ....

It should be noted that the words presented in the above examples might not always be the exact words that will appear on your exam script – e.g. you might find 'analyse', or 'outline' or 'investigate', etc. The best advice is to check over your past exam papers and familiarize yourself with the words that are most recurrent.

In summary, this section has been designed to give you reference points to measure where you are at in your studies, and to help you map out the way ahead in manageable increments. It should now be clear that learning should not merely be a mechanical exercise, such as just memorizing and reproducing study material. Quality learning also involves making connections between ideas, thinking at a deeper level by attempting to understand your material and developing a critical approach to learning. However, this cannot be achieved without the discipline of preparation for lectures, seminars and exams, or without learning to structure your material (headings and subheadings) and to set each unit of learning within its overall context in your subject and programme. An important device in learning is to develop the ability to ask questions (whether written, spoken or silent). Another useful device in learning is to illustrate your material and use examples that will help make your study fun, memorable and vivid. It is useful to set problems for yourself that will allow you to think through solutions and therefore enhance the quality of your learning.

On the one hand, there are the necessary disciplined procedures such as preparation before each learning activity and consolidation afterwards. It is also vital to keep your subject materials in organized folders so that you can add/extract/replace materials when you need to. On the other hand, there is the need to develop personality traits such as feeding your confidence, fuelling your motivation and turning stress responses to your advantage. This section has presented strategies to guide you through finding the balance between these organized and dynamic aspects of academic life.

Your aim should be to become an 'all-round student' who engages in and benefits from all the learning activities available to you (lectures, seminars, tutorials, computing, labs, discussions, library work, etc.), and to develop all the academic and personal skills that will put you in the driving seat to academic achievement. It will be motivating and confidence-building for you, if you can recognize the value of these qualities, both across your academic programme and beyond graduation to the world of work. They will also serve you well in your continued commitment to lifelong learning.

part four
essential resources

glossary

Absolute advantage
Goods that a nation can produce more efficiently than any other.

Acquisition
Where one company forcefully takes over another company.

Balance of Payment (BoP)
The accounting record of the transactions between a country and the rest of the world over a given period of time.

Benchmarking
A marketing technique that relies on the observation of competitors' management style to retain the best practices.

Bill of lading
A contract between the exporter and the transporter/carrier indicating the responsibility for the goods accepted by the logistics company that sells transportation in return for payment.

Bootlegging
The unauthorized recording of a musical broadcast on radio, television, or a live concert.

Born Global
Firms that are international by 'birth' in organization, structure and strategy.

Capital account
This states the long-term and short-term transactions like certificates of deposit or foreign exchange.

Cash flow management
This is about controlling money inflows and outflows so that the firm has enough resources for doing business at any moment in time.

Centralization

Where top managers make all decisions at headquarters while lower-level managers carry these directives out.

Centrally-determined economy

An economy that is controlled and directed by the state that creates policies and allocates the resources.

Change management

A discipline of management that uses knowledge, tools and resources to provide a particular business with a strategy for a period of organizational change within a company.

Civil law

Where the legal system judgement is based on an existing set of laws and rules defined by the legal power.

Common law

The legal system in which judges refer to the judgement made in previous cases to create or redefine the law.

Common market

Where there are no barriers to trade among members of this market grouping and there is a common external trade policy.

Comparative advantage

In the case that one nation produces two goods more efficiently than another, both parties still benefit from an exchange and should specialize in the production of the good for which they have the greatest relative advantage.

Competitive advantage

A sustainable advantage that a company enjoys over the competition.

Contract

An agreement that allows a firm to offer services abroad for a fee and for a certain period of time.

Contract management

Where the government keeps the ownership of assets but gives operational responsibilities to a private company.

Corporate culture	A set of norms, values and beliefs that are shared by the members of one company.
Cost leadership	A company's strategy that relies on cost reduction.
Counterfeiting	An unauthorized recording of pre-recorded sounds, or the duplication of original artwork, labels, trademarks, and packaging.
Current account	This states the monetary value of the international transactions in physical goods, in services, and in unilateral transfers such as gifts or aid.
Customs union	Where there are no barriers to trade among members and a common trade policy with respect to non-members.
Decentralization	Where decision-making in organizations is pushed down to the managers who are closest to the action, often the country managers.
Digital risk (high-tech risk)	A type of risk stemming from the information technology industry and depending on digital and cyber technologies; it deals with information theft or reluctant transfer, information disability, system destruction or infection.
Disaster management	A discipline of management dealing strictly with a type of critical occurrence that a company might face; the only certainty is that disasters will occur, but the timing and perhaps the periodicity is obscure.
Diversification	Where, in order to reduce the impact of exchange rate changes, the company spreads its assets and liabilities through several currencies (Euros, Dollars, etc.).
Divestiture	The selling of assets.

Double taxation

Where a company or person has to pay twice the income tax for the same source of revenue to the different countries in which it is operating.

Dumping

Where the export price of a product is under-average compared to the corresponding product, the 'like product', on foreign markets, under specific conditions.

Earned Value Analysis (EVA)

A crucial measure for any project; it gives an answer for the difference between real and estimated costs (before the start of the project) of a particular project; it can be carried out at any stage of the project realization.

Economic union

The integration of economic policies and the free movement of goods, services and factors of production.

Economies of scale

Where companies are able to reduce their production costs by increasing their quantities to supply a bigger market.

Embargo

The strongest trade sanctions that prohibit export (i.e. shipping) of particular goods to a country on which an embargo is placed.

Ethnocentrism

Where one believes one's culture to be superior to others.

Eurobonds

Bonds underwritten by an international syndicate of banks and other securities firms, and sold exclusively in countries other than the country whose currency denominates the issue.

Eurocurrency

A set of bank deposits located outside the countries whose currency is used in the deposit.

Euroequities	Shares of publicly traded stock whose primary exchange is located outside the issuing firm's home country.
Explicit knowledge	A category of knowledge that is codified and interacting information in databases, documents etc., and formalized.
Export commission agents	Overseas purchasers who buy for their foreign customers.
Export merchants	These buy goods directly from the producer and then sell, invoice and ship them in their own name.
Fiscal policy	One of the two major tools (the other is monetary policy) used by the government of a country to influence its economy (mostly: inflation, unemployment and production) by means of changes in taxation and/or government spending.
Foreign currency exposure management	A valuable tool for firms to protect themselves from fluctuations in the global currency price.
Foreign Direct Investment (FDI)	Where firms invest outside their home country and thus control their foreign assets.
Franchising	Where the use of trademarks or assets of a company is granted to an independent firm that pays a fee.
Free/liberal trade	Terms used for an economy or international trade pattern in which governments try to maximise the freedom of businesses exchange.
Free trade area	Where all barriers to trade among member countries are removed.

Global sourcing

The use of overseas suppliers and assembly plants.

Greenfield investment

Wholly owned investment that the firm retains for its own use.

Guanxi

A Chinese term which means 'informal, reciprocal obligation networks'; this is very important for business with China because the creation of relationships is the basis of future business success with Chinese business partners.

Hedging

Securing particular currency rates, thus safeguarding from future changes.

International value chain

A conceptual tool which is used to define the primary and secondary activities of one international company that determine the value added to a product or services.

Incoterms (International Commercial Terms)

Internationally accepted standard definitions, set by the International Chamber of Commerce, which are uniform for international shipment and sales activity.

Joint venture

Where two or more partners share a project that is limited in time, purpose and quantity.

Knowledge management (KM)

An evolution of information management and information technology that is directly related to corporate/strategic intelligence using specialized groupware, networking and business intelligence products that help firms develop, retain and transfer knowledge.

'Laissez-faire' economy

A liberal economy that is self-regulated and characterized by no or very few interventions of governments.

Letter of Credit	A document that guarantees that the issuing bank makes payments upon agreed terms, and the presentation of specific documents.
Licensing	This gives the right to use a product or concept or perform a service that is under intellectual property rights.
Macro political risk	A risk that affects all foreign enterprises in the same way.
Market driven economy	An economy that is self-regulated by the market and focus on customer demand to which companies try to respond the best by the right allocation of resources.
Mercantilism	The period from the 16th to the 18th centuries characterized by the encouragement of exports and stifling imports.
Merger	Where two or more full independent companies get together to form a new company.
Micro political risk	A risk that affects selected sectors of the economy or specific foreign businesses.
Monetary theory	One of the classical theories of macroeconomics giving the major economic influence to money demand and supply; using the core tools designed for controlling those two is crucial for dealing with issues such as inflation, unemployment or production.
Monopolistic competition	A market that is dominated by only one competitor which owns a large majority of the market share.
Nationalization	Where the government buys private goods or services that become a public property.
National systems of innovation	A system of clusters (private and public) responsible for R&D and innovation that are linked with

each other to reinforce the efficiency of innovations in a country; these include government, universities, and private companies.

Netting

Where before government reporting, international firms adjust and determine the net balance due to and from each separate operation.

Non-governmental organizations (NGOs)

Non-profit organizations which are focused on particular issues such as human rights, environmental protection and humanitarian work.

Non-tariff barrier

A restriction on imports that is imposed under certain conditions.

Pirating

An unauthorized duplication of sounds, images, etc., from a legitimate version.

Positive trade balance

Where both parties benefit from the exchange of goods or services between them.

Power distance

An index defined by Hofstede which measures the extent to which less powerful members of an organization or structure accept and consider the unequal distribution of power as a norm.

Privatization

Where the government sells public goods and services to private investors.

Product standardization

Products or services are similar in a variety of countries and the distinctions between these markets are low.

Purchase Power Parity

Describes how much one can buy with the home country's currency in another country with a different currency (it is a comparison of exchange rates and local prices).

Quotas	Limiting supply from foreign producers.
Return on Capital Employed (ROCE)	A financial tool for a ratio between Earnings Before Interest and Tax and Net Assets (total assets less current liabilities); it shows how much profit a company made thanks to its capital investments.
Return on Equity (ROE)	A tool used in finance; it is the ratio between net income and a shareholder's equity of a particular company; it gives information on how much profit a company made from money invested by its shareholders.
Risk adaptation	A strategy relying on the company's reactivity to risk occurrence.
Risk avoidance	A company decides not to enter a business or market to avoid the potential risk of doing so.
Risk transfer	The firm transfers the responsibility related to a specific risk to a third party that accepts the conditions.
Strategic alliance	Firms are working together on major strategic initiatives but cooperation is limited to a specific purpose.
Tacit knowledge	A category of knowledge stemming from people's intellect, intuition, education and experience; it is rather informal.
Tariffs	Tax levied on imports.
The Balanced Scorecard	A management tool that allows companies to manage knowledge, boost international strategy, corporate culture and control mechanisms and to evolve in this through the use of technology.
Trade creation	Beneficial results of companies trading more extensively with each other within the market group.

Trade diversion	A reduction of trade with companies outside the market group.
Trade policies	Policies designated to regulate, direct and protect national economic activity and welfare where necessary.
Trade sanctions	Trade penalties that countries impose against others. These include import tariffs, duties or licensing schemes.
Trading bloc	A preferential economic arrangement among a group of countries.
Transaction costs	Costs of an economic exchange.
Transfer pricing	The estimated cost of goods, services or funds transfer from one company to another related company.
Tax havens	Countries where tax rates are very low in comparison to others or do not exist at all.
Uncertainty avoidance	One of Hofstede's four dimensions for describing different cultures; it refers to a particular nation's acceptance or avoidance of doubtful situations.
Voluntary Export Restraints (VERs)	The importer limits shipping to a specific country, self-imposed and not due to tariffs and quotas that are, in contrast, imposed by governmental authorities.
Vulnerability	An objective estimation that the organizational system has features which constitute a high probability of adverse risks existing, and of subsequent development of crisis leading to disaster.

bibliography

Ajarimah, A. A. (2001) Major challenges of global leadership in the twenty-first century. *Human Resources Development International*, 4.

Bartlett, C., Ghoshal, S. and Brikinshaw, J. (2003) *Transnational Management*, 4th edition. McGraw-Hill.

Belch, G. and Belch, M. (1998) *Advertising and Promotion*, 4th edition. New York: Irwin and McGraw-Hill.

Bhagwati, J. (ed.) (1972) 'Economics and world order from the 1970s to the 1990s', in S. Hymer, *The Multinational Corporation and the Law of Uneven Development*. London: Macmillan.

Buckley, P. J., Burton, F. and Mrza, H. (1998) *The Strategy and Organization of International Business*. London: Macmillan.

Burenstam Linder, S. (1961) An Essay on Trade and Transformation Department of Economics. Stockholm: Stockholm School of Economics, Ph.D. p. 167

Bush, G.W. (2002) President Announces Tough New Enforcement Initiatives for Reform, Remarks by the President on Corporate Responsibility, 9 July, New York; http://www.whitehouse.gov/news/releases/2002/07/20020709-4. html

Butler, K. (2004) *Multinational Finance*, 3rd edition. Southwestern College Publishing.

Cateora, G. (2005) *International Marketing*, 12th edition. New York: McGraw-Hill.

Caves, R. (1998) 'Research on international business: problems and prospects', *Journal of International Business Studies*, 29: 5–19.

Certo, S. and Certo, S. (2005) *Modern Management*. New York: Prentice Hall.

Chapman, M. and Antoniou, C. (1994) *Uncertainty in Avoidance in Greece: An Ethnographic Illustration*. Indianapolis: Academy of International Business Annual Conference.

CNNmoney (1988) 'The big comeback at British Airways', http://money. cnn.com/magazines

CNNmoney (2000) 'French win $40B Orange', 30 May, http://money.cnn.com/2000

'Compliance Pipeline News, Financial Executives Call SOX Compliance A Good Investment: New Oversight Systems survey found many benefits to Sarbanes-Oxley compliance, but they come with a high cost'. 14 December, 2004, accessible on http://www.intelligententerprise.com/channels/business_intelligence/55800098

Cook, M. and Piggott, J. (1993) *International Business Economies*: A *European Perspective*, 2nd edition. London: Longman Group.

Czinkota, M. R., Ronkainen, I. A. and Moffett, M. H. (2005) *International Business*, 7th edition. Cincinnati: Thompson/Southwestern.

Czinkota, M. R., Ronkainen, I. A. and Moffett, M. H. (2007) *International Business*, 7th edition. Florence: Cengage Learning.

Daft, R. (2005) *The New Era of Management*, international edition. Mason: Thomson Learning/Southwestern.

Daft, R. (2005) *The New Era of Management*. Southwestern/Thomson Learning.

Dewenter, K., Higgins, R. and Simin, T. (2005) Can event study methods solve the currency exposure puzzle? Retrievable from ideas.repec.org/a/eee/pacfin/v13y2005i2p119-144.html

Dictionnaire de l´Economie (2000) Paris: Larousse/HER.

di Stefano, T. (2005) 'SOX: Europe Balks, US Bends', E-Commerce Times, 3 April, 5:00 AM PT, accessible on http://www.ecommercetimes.com/story/40905.html

Drucker, P. (2007) *People and Performance: The Best of Peter Drucker on Management*. Cambridge, MA: Harvard Business School Press.

Dunning, J. (1989) 'The study of international business: a plea for a more interdisciplinary approach', *Journal of International Business Studies*, 20: 411–36.

Ebbinghaus, H. http://www.web-us.com/MEMORY/hermann_ebbinghaus.htm

Eiteman, D. K., Stonehill, A. I. and Moffett, M. H. (2006) *Multinational Business Finance*, 11th edition. Upper Saddle River, NJ: Pearson Education.

Fisher, R. J. and Grenn, G. (2006) '*Specific Security Threats, 'Lock it or you'll lose it'*. Financial Times, 31, May.

Friedman, T.L. (2005) *The World is Flat: A Brief History of the Twenty-first Century*. New York: Macmillan.

Gancel, C. Rodgers, I. and Raynaud, M. (2002) *Successful Mergers, Acquisitions and Strategic Alliances: How to Bridge Corporate Cultures*. London and Boston: McGraw-Hill.

Ganzer, V. J. (1968) 'Effects of audience presence and test anxiety on learning and retention in a serial learning situation', *Journal of Personality and Social Psychology*, 8: 194–99.

Heckscher and Ohlin, in: B. Ohlin (1933) *Interregional and International Trade*. Cambridge, MA: Harvard University Press.

Hennart, J. F. (1991) 'The transaction cost theory of the multinational enterprise', in C. N. Pitelis and R. Strange (eds) *The Nature of the Transnational Firm*. London: Routledge.

Hill, C. (2002) *Global Business Today*, 2nd edition. New York: MacGraw-Hill.

Hill, C. (2008) *Global Business*, 7th edition. Boston: McGraw-Hill Higher Education.

Hofstede, G. (1996) *Cultures and Organizations, Software of the Mind: Intercultural Cooperation and its Importance for Survival*. London: McGraw-Hill.

Hofstede, G. (2001) *Culture's Consequences, Comparing Values, Behaviors, Institutions and Organizations Across Nations*, 2nd edition. Thousand Oaks, CA and London: Sage.

Hymer, S. (1960) 'The international operations of national firms: a study of direct investment', PhD thesis, MIT (published 1976).

InvestorWords (2006) The Law of One Price. Retrievable from www.investor-words.com

Johanson, J. and Wiedersheim-Paul, F. (1975) 'The internationalization of the firm-four Swedish cases', *Journal of Management Studies*, October, pp. 305–22.

Julius, D. (1994) 'International Direct Investment: Strengthening the Policy Regime' in P. Kenen (ed.) *Managing the World Economy: Fifty Years After Bretton Woods*. Washington DC: Institute for International Economics.

Kaplan, R. and Norton, D.P. (1992) 'The Balanced Scorecard: measures that drive performance', *Harvard Business Review*, January–February.

Kennedy, J.F. (1961) Inaugural Address, 20 January, Washington, D.C.

Kiam, V.(2007) www.risk-safety.admin.state.mn.us/.../Session7/negotiating (Negotiating Your Way to a Safer Minnesota, 2007 State Safety, Risk Management and Workers' Compensation Conference)

Krugman, P. (1980) Scale Economies, Product Differentiation, and the Pattern of Trade, *The American Economic Review*, 70 (5) Dec.: 950–59.

Luchins, A. S. (1942) 'Mechanisms in problem solving: the effects of *Einstellung*', *Psychological Monographs*, 54 (248).

Marshall, A., Faff, R. and Nguyen, H. (2006) Exchange rate exposure, foreign currency derivatives and the introduction of the Euro: French evidence. Retrievable from www.fma.org/Siena/Papers.

Marx, K. (1867/1894) *Capital* (Das Kapital, edited by F. Engels). New York and Moscow: Progress Publishers and International Publishers (first English edition 1887).

McAlister, D., Ferrell, O. and Ferrell, L. (2005) *Business and Society: A Strategic Approach to Social Responsibility*, 2nd edition. Boston: Houghton Mifflin.

McIlroy, D. (2003) *Studying at University: How to be a Successful Student*. London: Sage.

McIntyre, J. and Travis, E. (2006) Global supply chain under conditions of uncertainty: economic impacts, corporate responses, strategic lessons. In G. Suder (ed.) *Corporate Strategies Under International Adversity*. Cheltenham: E. Elgar Publications.

Mill, J.S. (1848, book III 1891) *Principles of Political Economy*. New York: D. Appleton & Co.

Morosini, P. (1998) *Managing Cultural Differences: Effective Strategy and Execution Across Cultures in Global Corporate Alliances*. Oxford: Pergamon Press.

Mühlbacher, H., Leihs, H. and Dahringer, L. (2006) *International Marketing: A Global Perspective*, 3rd edition. London: Thompson Learning.

Porter, M. (1998) *Competitive Advantage: Creating and Sustaining Superior Advantage*. New York: Free Press.

Pritamani, M., Shome , D.K., Singal, V. (2003) Foreign Exchange Exposure of Exporting and Importing Firms, Working paper series, Available at SSRN: http://ssrn.com/abstract=429860 or DOI: 10.2139/ssrn.429860

Punnett, B. and Ricks, D. (1998) *International Business*, 2nd edition. Blackwell.

Ricardo, D. (1817) *On the Principles of Political Economy and Taxation*. London: John Murray

Rowley, J. (2000) 'Learning organization to knowledge entrepreneur', *Journal of Knowledge Management*, 4 (Jan): 7–14.

Rugman, A. and Brewer, T. (eds) (2003) *The Oxford Handbook of International Business*. Oxford: Oxford University Press.

Rugman, A. and Collinson, S. (2006) *International Business*, 4th edition. London: Financial Times Prentice-Hall.

Rugman, A. and Hodgetts R (1995) *International Business*. New York: McGraw-Hill.

Rugman, A. and Hodgetts R. (2002), *International Business: A Strategic Management Approach,* 3rd edition. Englewood: FT Prentice Hall.

Samuelson, P.A. (1947) *Foundations of Economic Analysis*. Cambridge, MA: Harvard Economics Studies 80.

Santos-Paulino, A. U. (2005) 'Trade liberalisation and economic performance: theory and evidence for developing countries', *The World Economy*, 28(6): 783–821.

Schein, E. (2004) *Organizational Culture and Leadership*, 3rd edition. New York: Wiley Publishers.

Shenkar, O. (2004) 'One more time: international business in a global economy', *Journal of International Business Studies*, 35(2): 161–71.

Sherman, P. J. and Helmreich, R. L. (1996) Attitudes toward automation. In Proceedings of the Eighth International Symposium on Aviation Psychology. Columbus, OH: Ohio State University.

Showers, B. (1984). Peer coaching: A strategy for facilitating transfer of training. Eugene, Center for Educational Policy and Management, Oregon.

Smith, A. (1776) *The Wealth of Nations*. London: Penguin Books.

Spradley, J. (1979) *The Ethnographic Interview*. Wadsworth Group/Thomas Learning.

Stiglitz, J. (2002) *Globalization and Its Discontents*. New York: W.W. Norton.

Suder, G. (Ed.) (2004) *Terrorism and the International Business Environment: The Business – Security Nexus*. Cheltenham: E. Elgar Publications. See www.e-elgar.com

Suder, G. (Ed.) (2006) *Corporate Strategies Under International Adversity.* Cheltenham: E. Elgar Publications. See www.e-elgar.com

Transparency International (2007) Global Corruption Report and transparency international Malaysia Report, http://www.transparency.org

Trompenaars, F. and Hampden-Turner, C. (1998) *Riding the Waves of Culture: Understanding Cultural Diversity in Global Business,* 2nd edition. New York: McGraw-Hill.

Vernon, R. (1994) 'Contributing to an international business curriculum: an approach from the flank', *Journal of International Business Studies,* 25: 215–27.

Viner, J. (1926) *A Memorandum on Dumping.* Geneva: League of Nations.

Wei, E. (2006) Transaction exposure. Retrievable from utminers.utep.edu/zwei/Fin4325/esmCh08.ppt

Wolf, M. (2004) *Why Globalization Works: The Case for the Global Economy.* New Haven, CT: Yale University Press.

Zhao, L., Yim-Teo, T.H. and Yeo, K.T. (2004) Knowledge management issues in outsourcing. Engineering Management Conference Proceedings, October. *IEEE International,* 2(18–21): 541–45.

appendix of useful websites

EUROSTAT – epp.eurostat.ec.europa.eu The publication of European Union statistics on all trade, business- and economy-related issues that involve Europe, by far or by long.

The Federation of International Trade Associations (FITA) – www.fita.org Although some of the content here is for sale, there are many useful links found on the FITA site. Business directories, cultural information on different countries, links to glossaries and dictionaries, lists of government and multinational organizations, and several forums for trading information are among the many things to be found here.

The Global Edge – globaledge.msu.edu/resourceDesk/ International business and global trade resources and many academic sources, with many useful links to even more resource sites.

The International Trade Center (ITC) – www.intracen.org Extensive dossiers by individual countries can be found on the ITC site. The age of the data depends on the selected country, but was found to be fairly recent (2004–2005). Information such as trade performance indexes, national export performance, import profiles and even statistic reliability for the figures is provided. Most of the content is also free of charge.

The World Bank – www.worldbank.org Reports, data and a multitude of insights into international trade and development issues, on topic or country perspective, indicators for markets, economies and a variety of other themes, with key reports, numbers and figures.

The World Trade Organization (WTO) – www.wto.org The WTO provides extensive information on worldwide import and export statistics. The latest data is from 2005, so is quite recent, and can be requested free of charge. Precise numbers on amounts traded or percentiles can be collected either by regions, countries, imports, exports and trade sectors.

index

Note: page numbers in **bold** indicate a glossary entry

absolute advantage
    18–20, **180**
'acceptance zones' 96
accounting compliance 52–3
acquisitions 59–60, **180**
After Action Review
    (AAR) 101
Anglo-Saxon business
    model 105
Ansoff matrix 68
arbitration 36
Aristotle 113
arm's length price 54
Army Business
    Transformation
    Center 111
Asia
    Flying Geese model 64–5
    see also China; India
Association of Southeast
    Asian Nations (ASEAN)'s
    AFTA 44
Aulotte, J.-M. 101
autonomic nervous system
    155, 163

Balance of Payment (BoP)
    41, **180**
Balanced Scorecard, The
    104–7, **188**
'Banana War' 41
Bangladesh 97
BCG (Boston Consulting
    Group) matrix 68
Belch, G. 85
Belch, M. 85
benchmarking 68, **180**
best practice 102
bilateral relations 40
Bills of Lading 79, **180**
black holes 74
BMW 102
Bon, M. 102
bootlegging 90, **180**
Born Globals 13, 60, **180**
boycotts 120
Bretton Woods 48, 55
BRIC countries (Brazil,
    Russia, India, China) 64

burglary 90
Burma 119
Bush, G.W. 37
business law 36
business operations 10, 75–81
Butler, K. 51

Canada 96, 117
capital account 41, **180**
capital market rulers 54–5
CARICOM (Central American
    Common Market) 44
cash flow management 54,
    180
Cateora, G. 80
Caves, R. 4
centralization 73, **181**
centrally-determined
    economies 32, **181**
change management
    110–11, **181**
Chief Financial Officers
    (CFOs) 87
China
    Guanxi 97
    inclusion in triad 43
    market entry service
        providers 82
    mercantilist trend 18
    product/service balance 81
    supplier agreements 5
    trade surplus 41
civil law 34, **181**
civil society 37, 118
climate change 14, 114
cloth trade 20
collegial coaching 101
Collinson, S. 65, 82
common law 34, **181**
common market 44, **181**
comparative advantage 20–1,
    40, **181**
    and knowledge
        management 105–6
comparative business studies 4
competitive advantage **181**
    and confidentiality 25
    and knowledge
        management 101

competitive advantage *cont.*
    Porter's Diamond 25, 43
    and strategic audit 67
Competitive Clusters 25
competitive moves 71
Compliance Pipeline News 53
contract management 32, **181**
contracts 59, **181**
contributors 74
cooperative exporters 59
Corporate Social
    Responsibility (CSR) 38
corporate culture 27, 29, **182**
    and international
        strategy 70
    valuing diversity 30
corruption 14–15, 96–7
cost leadership 70, **182**
cost of living allowance
    (COLA) 63
counterfeiting 90, **182**
country attractiveness, 2 x 2
    matrix 68
country risk analysis 89
Courtois, J.-P. 104
cultural dimensions
    theories 30–1
culture 9, 26–31
    and ethics 37
    and market assessment 81
    and uncertainty 88, 96–7
currency
    basic concepts 48–9
    exposure management 50,
        51–2
    exposure types 50–1
current account 41, **182**
customs unions 44, **182**
Czinkota, M. R. 13, 61, 69, 71,
    79, 82, 84

Daimler Chrysler 28
decentralization 73, **182**
    coordinated 73
decision-making
    organizations 73
Dell Theory of Conflict
    Prevention 91
democracies 17, 32

Denmark 97
developing countries/
　less-developed countries
　(LDCs)
　benefits of globalization
　115
　fair trade 15
　Flying Geese model 64–5
　free trade risks 40
　intragroup trade 121
　trade liberalization 39
　transparency problems 97
　World Bank role 116
Dewenter, K. 52
di Stefano, T. 53
Diamond of National
　Advantage 25, 43
Dictionnaire de L'Economie
　112
differentiation 70
digital (high-tech) risk
　88–9, **182**
disaster management 98–9,
　182
distribution 84–5
diversification 51, **182**
divestiture 32, **182**
division of labour 19, 20
double taxation 53, **183**
Dow Jones Sustainability
　Index 38
Drucker, P. 101
Duisenberg, W. 45
dumping 83–4, **183**
Dunning, J. 4, 58

Earned Value Analysis (EVA)
　105, **183**
East African Community
　(EAC) 44
Ebbinghaus, H. 151
e-commerce 86
Economic Espionage Act
　(1996) 90
economic integration 10, 33,
　39–46
economic union 44–5, **183**
economic/white collar crime
　89–90
economies of scale 24, 62,
　109, **183**
　external 34
　internal 33–4
embargoes 120, **183**
employment law 36
England 20
espionage 90
essay writing 134–43
　adversarial system 136
　evidence and sources
　140–1
　finding major questions
　139–40

essay writing *cont.*
　introduction 142
　key concepts 135–6
　quotations 141
　structuring and outline 138–9
　tributary principle 135
essay/exam questions 165–77
　analysing the parts 170–1
　'compare and contrast'
　　questions 174–5
　critical approach 169
　interpreting the question
　166
　learning sets 171–2
　missing your question 168
　relevance 166–7
　visual illusions 165–6
　writing down 168–9
ethics 37–8, 111–12
ethnocentrism 28, **183**
Eurobonds 55, **183**
Eurocurrency 54–5, **183**
Euroequities 55, **184**
Europe
　mercantilism 18
　Organization for Security
　　and Co-operation
　　(OSCE) 116–17
　small and medium
　　enterprises
　　dominant 13
　　and SOX regulations 53
　　stakeholder model 105
European Commission
　(CEC) 60
European Community 117
European Union 6
　customs union with
　　Turkey 44
　economic union 45
　goals 46
　Incoterms 80
　Rome Convention 35
　export legislation 120
　triad economy 43
EUROSTAT 195
exams 7, 38, 155–64
　archery analogy 63–4
　links to revision 161–2
　'name dropping' 163
　practical details 159–60
　sample questions 12, 32,
　　45, 50, 74, 80, 91,
　　110–11
　task management 158–9
　time management 156–8
　see also essay/exam
　　questions
exchange rates 47 *see also*
　currency
expatriates 63–4
explicit knowledge 100, 103,
　107–8, **184**

export commission agents
　59, **184**
export documentation 78–9
export merchants 59, **184**
export pricing 83
exports 59
　embargoes 120
Exxon Mobil 56

factor proportions 21–2
fair trade 15
Federation of International
　Trade Associations (FITA)
　118, **195**
Finland 97
first-mover advantage 57, 77
fiscal policy 113, **184**
Flying Geese model 64–5
focus 70
Ford 28
foreign currency exposure
　management 50, 51–2,
　184
Foreign Direct Investment
　(FDI) 43–4, 60, 89, **184**
foreign market pricing 83
Foreign Trade Zones 80
forward rate buying 49
Frankfurt InterBank Offered
　Rate (PIBOR) 55
France 6, 18, 117
franchising 58, **184**
free/liberal trade 28, 39–40,
　119, **184**
　and economic wealth 17
　Smith's advocacy 19
free trade areas 44, **184**
Friedman, T. L. 91
fronting loans 54
funds positioning techniques 54

G7/G8 117
Gandhi, M. 120
Ganzer, V. J. 160
Gates, B. 60, 112
General Agreement on Tariffs
　and Trade (GATT) 39,
　40, 117
General Motors 96
geopolitics 118–21
Germany 29, 117
Global Edge 195
global sourcing 75, **185**
global terrorism 87, 90
globalization 9, 11–12
　benefits for developing
　　world 115
　and corporate law boom 34
　and cultural
　　understanding 27
　Guanxi 97
　and the monetary system
　　10, 47–55

globalization *cont.*
  positive/negative effects
    11–12, 24
  and risk 10
  and role of international
    organizations and
    NGOs 121–2
  and supply chain
    management 92
GLOBE 31
'glocalisation' 71
Gold Standard 48
good practice 102
government-business
  cooperation 32–3
Great Britain *see* UK/Great
  Britain
greenfield investment 60, **185**
Guanxi 97, **185**

Hague-Vishy Rules on Bills of
  Lading 34
Haiti 97
Heckscher, E. 21–2
hedging 49, 51–2, **185**
Hennart, J. F. 4
Hill, C. 32, 71, 76, 77–8
Hitachi 71
H-O model 21–2, 23
Hodgetts, R. 60
Hofstede, G. 26, 28, 31, 88
human resources (HR) 62–4
Hymer, S. 4, 60

IBM Lotus Notes 103
identity theft 88
IKEA 70
implementors 74
Incoterms (International
  Commercial terms) 34,
  79–80, 94, **185**
independent study 126–7
independent suppliers 77
India
  corruption 97
  inclusion in triad 43
  product/service balance 81
  trade surplus 41
Indonesia 97
Information and
  Communication
  Technology (ICT) 14
information sources 7–8
in-groups 27
innovation 25, 77
Intellectual Property Rights 36
internal analysis 69–70
internal fund flows 54
International Bank for
  Reconstruction and
  Development (IBRD) 116
international business
  basics 9, 11–16
  definition 5

international business *cont.*
  history 4
  studying 6–7
  thinking like a manager 3–6
International Chamber of
  Commerce 34, 36, 79
International Court of
  Arbitration 36
International Development
  Association (IDA) 116
international economy
  112–22
International Institute for the
  Unification of Private
  Law 34
international institutions 10,
  114–18
  influence of globalization
    121–2
international investment
  theory 25–6
international market
  assessment 81
International Monetary Fund
  (IMF) 15, 48, 55, 115, 122
international strategy 10,
  66–71
international trade 13, 16–17,
  61
  and international economy
    112–22
international trade and
  investment theory 4, 9,
  16–26
International Trade Center
  (ITC) 118, 195
international trading
  companies 59
international values 21
internationalization 10, 12,
  43, 56–65
  and change management 111
  stages model 4
internationalization process 56
internet 14, 74
  internet-sold services 86
  see also digital risk
intracompany pricing 83
inventory buffer 93
Invisible Hand 19
Italy 20–1, 29, 53, 117

Japan
  Flying Geese leader 64, 65
  Fuji-Xerox 24
  G7/G8 117
  quality management 108
  triad economy 43
joint ventures 59, 185
Just in Time inventory 76

Kennedy, J. F. 96
KFC 58
Kiam, V. 94

knowledge 100 *see also*
  explicit knowledge; tacit
  knowledge
knowledge management
  (KM) 10, 99–112, 185
Krugman, P. 24

labour disputes 90
labour law 36
labour theory of value 19, 21
Lafarge 101
laissez-faire economy 19, 185
large enterprises (LEs) 13
law 9, 34–7
Law of One Price 49
'Learning and Growth
  Perspectives' 106
learning links 131–2
lectures 124–8
  context 124
  developing 127–8
  and independent study 126–7
  note-taking strategy 127
  notes (provided by
    lecturer) 124–5
  technical terms 125–6
Leontief paradox 23
less-developed countries *see*
  developing countries
Letters of Credit 79, **186**
liberalization *see* trade
  liberalization
licensing 58, **186**
limited liability companies 35
Linder, S. B. 24
localization 56–7
logistics 78–80
  risks 94
London InterBank Offered
  Rate (LIBOR) 55
Luchins, A. S. 171

macro political risk 89, **186**
Madrid terrorist attacks 94
management
  Drucker's definition 101
  foreign currency exposure
    50, 51–2
  local vs. foreign 57
  role in internalization
    56, 61–2
  see also knowledge
    management
manufacturing strategy 75–6
marginal utility 19–20
market and competitive
  analysis 69
market concentration 85
market convergence 12
market diversification 85
market-driven economies 16,
  32, **186**
market entry service
  providers 82

marketing strategy 81–5
  '4 Ps' 82–5
  'glocalisation' 71
Marshal, C. 110
Marx, K. 21
Marxian economics 19
McDonald's 58
McKinsey/GE matrix 68
McKinsey growth pyramid 69
McKinsey's Global Survey 15
mercantilism 18, **186**
MERCOSUR 44
mergers 59–60, **186**
Mexico 96
micro political risk 89, **186**
Microsoft 60, 104
Middle East 29
Mill, J. S. 21, 113
mixed economies 32
mnemonics 149–51
modes of entry 58–60
monetary system 10, 47–55
monetary theory 113, **186**
monopolistic competition 24,
  26, **186**
Morosini, P. 28
Mühlbacher, H. 81
multiculturalism 27–8
multidisciplinary approach 4
multilateral netting 54
multilateral relations 40
multinational
  companies/enterprises
  (MNCs/MNEs)
  definition 60
  transactional companies
    distinguished 12, 57
Mundell, R. 47

NAFTA 96
national systems of
  innovation 107, **186–7**
nationalization 32, **186**
negotiation risks 94–6
  MNE/government 95, 96
  partners 96
  MNEs 95, 96
negotiations, and cultural
  differences 29
netting 51, **187**
  multilateral 54
network theory 24
New Trade Theory 24
New Zealand 97
non-governmental
  organizations (NGOs)
  10, 114, **187**
  and boycotts 120
  and company citizenship 37
  and Global Environment
    Facility of the World
    Bank 116
  influence of globalisation
    121–2

non-tariff barriers 39, **187**
North American Free Trade
  Agreement (NAFTA) 44
North Atlantic Treaty
  Organisation (NATO) 117
'not-invented-here'
  syndrome 74

Ohlin, B. 21–2
OLI (ownership, location and
  internalization)
  paradigm 58
olive oil export 20–1
Organization for Economic
  Cooperation and
  Development (OECD)
  15, 39, 116
Organization for Security
  and Co-operation in
  Europe (OSCE) 116–17
organizational structures
  71–5
  global area 72
  global functional 72–3
  global hybrid 73
  global matrix 73
  global product 72
  international divisions 72
out-groups 27
outsourcing 109–10
  supply chain 93
overlapping product ranges
  theory 24

packaging 78
Palmolive 28
Paris InterBank Offered Rate
  (PIBOR) 55
Parker Pen 28
pasta export 20–1
PEST risk analysis 89
PESTEL analysis 67
Pharmacia and Upjohn 28
photocopier life cycle 24
pirating 90, **187**
place (distribution) 84–5
political economy 10, 13, 31–2
  impact of geopolitics 118–21
  and international
    business 113
  international complexity 39
political risk 31, 89–91
politics 9, 31–4 *see also*
  geopolitics
Porter, M. 25, 69
Porter's Diamond 25, 43
Porter's Five Forces 67, 68
portfolio investment 44
Portugal 20
positive trade balance 18, **187**
power distance 31, **187**
presentations 133–4
price coordination 83
pricing 82–4

Private International Law 35
privatization 32, **187**
proactive firms 61
  motivations for
    internalization 62
product/s
  customization decision 70
  local assembly and
    packaging 59
  local adaptation 57, 67, 82
  standardization 67, **187**
product liability 35–6
product life cycle theory
  4, 23–4
product/service balance 80–1
production
  factor proportions theory
    21–2
  globalization 12
  integration 76–7
  localization 57
  location decision 76
productivity approach 18
profits, and localization 57
project management 108
promotion 85
protectionism 33, 40, 119
Public International Law 35
Purchase Power Parity (PPP)
  49, **187**

quality management 107–8
quotas 133, **188**
quotations 141

Radio Frequency
  Identification
  Technology (RFID) 93
reactive firms 61
  motivations for
    internationalization 62
referencing 141
regionalism 9, 12
research and development
  (R&D) 77–8
  delocalization 98
  digital risk prevention 88–9
  government-business
    cooperation 32–3
Return on Capital Employed
  (ROCE) 105, **188**
Return on Equity (ROE)
  104–5, **188**
revision 144–54
  alternating methods 151–3
  confidence booster 151
  good study habits 154
  mnemonics 149–51
  with others 153
  record keeping 146–7
  'revisiting' 144
  summary notes 145–6
  throughout the course 144–5
  using past papers 148–9

Ricardo, D. 20–1
risk adaptation 50, **188**
risk avoidance 50, **188**
risk management 97–8
risk transfer **188**
risks 10, 87–99
  currency 50–1
  digital 88–9, **182**
  external 88
  internal 88
  negotiation 94–6
  political 31, 89–91
  supply chain 91–4
  uncertainties contrasted 87
robbery 90
Rome Convention 35
Rousseau, J. J. 113
Rugman, A. 60, 65, 70, 82,
  85, 99, 107, 118
Russia 64, 117

'safe-haven' countries 93
Samuelson, P. 22
Sarbanes-Oxley (SOX)
  regulations 53
Schein, E. 27
scope 34
seminars 129–34
  complementary nature 130
  contributing 132–4
  creating the right climate
    130–1
  importance 129
  learning links and
    transferable skills
    131–2
service/product balance
  80–1
services 86
shareholder model 37, 105
Shenkar, O. 5
small- and medium-sized
  enterprises (SMEs) 13, 60
Smith, A. 17, 18–20, 64
South Africa 96
South Korea 40, 65
Spain 20–1, 29
Special Drawing Right
  (SDR) 55
specialization 18, 64
Spradley, J. 26
stakeholder diversity 14
stakeholder model 37, 105
'stand-alone' services 86
Stiglitz, J. E. 24–5, 115
storage 80
strategic alliances 59, **188**
strategic audit 67
strategic leaders 74
strategic planning process
  69–71
Suder, G. 87
supply chain risks 91–4
Supply Chain Visibility 93

sustainable development
  111–12
SWOT analysis 68

tacit knowledge 100, 103,
  107–8, **188**
Taiwan 40, 65
tariffs 33, 39, **188**
tax havens 54, **189**
taxation, international
  53–4, 62
technical terms 125–6
technology 13–14
  digital risk prevention 88–9
  knowledge management
    102–4
  supply chain
    management 94
terrorism 87, 90–1, 93, 94
Texas Instruments 71
totalitarian regimes 32
Toyota 96
trade barriers 33, 62, 119
  reduction/abolition 39
trade creation 33, 45, **188**
trade diversion 33, 45, **189**
trade liberalization 39–40
trade policies 17, **189**
trade relations 10, 39–46
trade sanctions 119–20, **189**
trading blocs 44, **189**
training 102, 106
transaction costs 4, 57, **189**
transfer pricing 54, **189**
transferable skills 131–2
transnational companies
  (TNCs) 12, 57
transparency 97
Transparency International
  14–15
transportation 78–80
  risks 94
treaties 35
triad countries 43
  emerging markets 66
  Foreign Direct
    Investment 44
  mergers and acquisitions 60
  product/service balance
    80–1
Trompenaars, F. 31
Turkey 44
'turn-key' operations 59

UK/Great Britain
  G7/G8 117
  Gold Standard
    abandoned 48
  information security
    costs 88
  Rank-Xerox 24
uncertainties 10, 87–99
  cultural causes 96–7
  risks contrasted 87

uncertainty avoidance
  88, 189
Uncertainty Avoidance Index
  (UAI) 88
Unilever 71
United Automobile Workers 96
United Nations (UN) 115
  Commission on
    International Trade
    Law 34
  Convention on Contracts
    for International Sales
    of Goods 35
  Framework Convention on
    Climate Change 114
  Industrial Development
    Organization
    (UNIDO) 15
Uppsala internationalization
  school 4
USA
  'Banana War' 41
  G7/G8 117
  Gold Standard
    abandoned 48
  Leontief paradox 23
  Partnership Act (1890) 35
  product liability cases 35
  product life cycles 23–4
  SOX regulations 53
  tax regulations 53
  trade sanctions 119–20
  triad economy 43
  UN ratification 35

value-added activities,
  location 71
value chain 25, 58, 67
Vernon, R. 4, 23–4
Viner, J. 83–4
visual illusions 165–6
Voluntary Export Restraints
  (VERs) 33, **189**
vulnerability 87, **189**
  supply chain 91–2

Wal-Mart 46
Wealth of Nations, The 18,
  19, 20
websites 195
Wei, E. 50
wine trade 20
Wolf, M. 64
World Bank 115, 116, 122, 195
World Economic Forum 15, 114
World Intellectual Property
  Organization (WIPO) 90
World Trade Organization
  (WTO) 39, 40, 86, 96,
  117, 118, 119, 122

Xerox 24

Yellow Pages 101, 103